S0-AQI-846

LIFE TOUCHED WITH WONDER

LIFE TOUCHED WITH WONDER

The BLESSINGS *of* NATURE

FROM THE EDITORS OF READER'S DIGEST

THE READER'S DIGEST ASSOCIATION, INC.
PLEASANTVILLE, NEW YORK

ISBN 0-7621-8872-3

Printed in the United States of America

Book design by Patrice Sheridan

You can also visit us on the World Wide Web at http://www.rd.com

CONTENTS

INTRODUCTION

When one tugs at a single thing in nature, he finds it attached to the rest of the world.

— John Muir

We feel awe when we see a grand landscape or view the majesty of a starry sky. But there's also wonder in a child's kiss when you're feeling down, in a friend's unexpected recovery from a frightening illness, in a walk on a hushed, snowy night. Such moments take us by surprise and lift us from the mundane and the familiar. Suddenly, inexplicably, we catch a glimpse of a reality beyond ourselves, and see evidence that there is something beautiful, merciful, loving knit into the fabric of creation—even in ourselves.

In fact, ordinary people can be the most gifted messengers of wonder. Their stories offer compelling evidence of the power of the spirit in daily life. In this new book series we have selected the best of such true-life stories and present them in separate volumes organized around themes.

In *The Blessings of Nature* you will find stories that illuminate the remarkable connections among people, the natural world, and the creatures who share it with us. These heartwarming stories show that the world around us can be a great teacher, inspiring us with the eternal lessons of courage, friendship, and perseverance.

A HUMMINGBIRD'S MAGIC

BY
NORMA LEE BROWNING

There is no use mincing words: My husband is legally blind. His sight loss is due to diabetic retinopathy, a progressive disease usually considered irreversible. It struck his older sister, too; we knew what to expect.

I remember the day several years ago when Russell came home from the doctor's office and gently broke the news to me. Doctors and hospitals had been a way of life for us since his first diabetic coma in 1942. He had survived numerous complications of diabetes, and adjusted to the daily insulin regimen. Always he rebounded from a crisis with a smile.

But there was no smile now as he said, "It means I'm finished as a photographer. I'd rather lose a leg than my eyes. That's one thing I can't take."

Neither can I, I thought. We began a frantic search for anything in medical science that might save his sight. The only hope, we were told, was a series of laser-beam operations, but it was chancy. We took the chance. Although the operations have caused considerable secondary visual-field loss, they probably resulted in saving the little usable central vision Russell has today.

I remember the shock of seeing the black eye-patches for the first time when I picked him up at the hospital. But more shocking was the despair I could feel gripping him as he clung to my arm and let me lead him to the car. I could face his loss of sight far better than his loss of spirit.

For five years our life was a succession of black eye-patches. Diminishing budget. Bouts of eye hemorrhaging, during which he had almost no vision.

Russell stumbled and groped his way around our Palm Springs, California, house and yard, adamantly rejecting such options as Braille, a Seeing Eye dog, retraining programs. "I don't need them yet. Maybe I won't lose my sight completely, maybe it will come back." The exotic canes that friends brought him he tucked away in the closet. He bought a pair of dark glasses, but threw them out.

Then it was spring 1974. We were sitting on the front patio. He was at his lowest ebb, doing something he had always said he would never do—just sitting and staring into space.

I knew what he was thinking: he was finished as a photographer, a has-been. He had sold most of his camera equipment. "I don't need it anymore, and we can use the money." I choked back tears, desperate to think of something to cheer him.

At that moment we heard a whirring of wings and a tiny bird zipped past us, spun around, and hovered, his wings beating so rapidly that I could barely see them.

"It's a hummingbird!" Russell said.

"How do you know?" He could see light, some colors, blurred images directly in front of him, and that was all.

"I can hear it."

The bird zoomed straight at Russell's head, put on his brakes inches in front of his face, and hung there as though suspended by an invisible thread. "Hello, little hummingbird," Russell said softly. "Where did you come from, pretty bird? Are you hungry?"

Russell could distinguish flashes of the brilliant red of the hummingbird's head and throat feathers glittering in the sunlight. The hummer darted and dived, spinning spectacular aerial acrobatics, bzee-bzeeing in our ears.

In the ensuing days, my husband developed a rapport with Little Redbird, as we named him. Russell no longer sat and stared. His eyes were galvanized on the feeder he made for the hummer and a bird-shooter he was building to photograph him.

The bird-shooter was an ingenious improvisation of leftovers from his photo workshop and "junkbox." He adapted an old Speed Graphic lens to an early-vintage 35 mm. camera he had bought in Hong Kong 25 years before and wouldn't part with; but the 35 mm. was too small for him to work with so we bought a new camera. Otherwise, most of his bird-shooter was his own design.

Life has a way of telescoping certain misfortunes of the past into extra dividends for the future. Russell had never been one to waste time in a hospital; he was always doing or learning something—practicing the cello, tying trout flies, repairing cameras. During one of his early month-long interludes at Northwestern Memorial Hospital in Chicago, he had completed a six-month course in electronics. Thus he knew how to build an electric-eye door opener.

He now transferred this knowledge to photographing hummingbirds. When the birds flew in front of the camera lens, they broke a light beam that triggered the shutter. Russell was soon photographing hummingbirds without being able to see them—or, rather, they were photographing themselves.

He did everything by touch-and-feel. "It's a matter of applying your other senses," he explained. "People forget that there's a lot of usable stuff up here between our two ears besides eyes."

Meanwhile, other hummingbirds came. He learned to recognize them by chirps, buzzing, wing-whirs, behavior antics. But Little Redbird remained his favorite—and the most elusive on camera.

"I'll get him eventually," Russell told me. "It just takes patience." He had a new purpose, a greater challenge than anything he had ever attempted when he had normal vision. He actually seemed happier than I had ever known him to be.

Russell's enthusiasm was contagious. I soon became hooked on hummingbirds, too. I bought some bird books and decided our Little Redbird was probably a male Anna's (*Calypte anna*), the only U.S. hummer with both a red crown and throat. I learned that experts have been driven nearly to despair trying to photograph hummingbirds. The odds against a photographer catching one on film are 30 to one!

When I relayed this news to Russell, his comment was, "Hmmm. I'm doing better than that." He was averaging one in 15.

Hummingbirds fuss and feud with one another, but are astonishingly unafraid of humans, as Little Redbird evidently was. They can do things in flight that no other bird can do, and have peculiar habits of courting, nesting, and feeding (every ten minutes). When they go to sleep, they become torpid to conserve energy. Early missionaries in South America, habitat of most hummingbird species, used the "awakening of the hummingbirds" to explain the Resurrection.

When I read this I had an eerie feeling. How strange that Russell's awakening from torpor, his resurrection from a dark tunnel, should begin with a hummingbird.

I began taking Russell's best pictures to be framed to hang in our dinette, which I named the Hummingbird Room. Framers and shop clerks would ask, "Who made these pictures? Are they for sale?" Word spread, and hummingbirders came by to see how Russell did it.

An artist friend, John Morris, dropped by one day and told him, "You're doing something very unusual. You should think about having an exhibit. This one, for example—it looks like an abstract painting."

"That's one of my mistakes," Russell said. "One of my strobes didn't go off."

"Some of an artist's best works are mistakes," John said.

A few days later, gallery owner Kay Obergfel came over. Her eyes darted over the pictures. "They're stunning," she said. "I don't know anything about photography. But I *do* know art. I'm going to exhibit these birds."

A bird does not sing because it has an answer. It sings because it has a song.

CHINESE PROVERB

Our immediate problem was to get enough pictures—35 to 40—printed, signed, numbered, and framed in four months. Once Russell could have turned out 100 color prints in a day. Now he was lucky to do one a week. Many of those already framed were in his opinion not good enough, and if he didn't like them he wouldn't sign them. They landed in his pile of rejects.

His Little Redbird print, the only picture he had of our first hummer, was one he refused to show. "Photographically it's terrible," he said. "I'll get a better one soon."

But one day Little Redbird flew over our oleanders, streaking toward the mountains, and never came back. I have a secret theory that it was part of the miracle he hatched—making a man strain his eye muscles looking for him.

I enlisted the help of a friend, Caroline Rogers. She came by regularly and cudgeled Russell into signing the rejects on the pretense that she wanted them for her own collection. She would then drop them off at the framer's for me on her way home. "Hummingbirds: Self-Portraits" opened Easter weekend 1977, and the exhibit was a success beyond our wildest dreams.

The most astonished guests were his two doctors, Doctor Burton J. Winston, his internist, and Doctor Kenneth A. Grow, his ophthalmologist. Said Doctor Grow, "Knowing the condition of his eyes as well as I do—the optic areas that have been destroyed, the visual-field loss—I can't explain medically how he is able to do this. I think the answer has to come from within, from inspiration, the desire and will to do something. We can grade the amount of visual acuity. But there is no way to grade inspiration."

I realized then the meaning of the miracle Little Redbird had brought us: the gift of vision without sight.

There seems to be no end to the marvels, great and small, unleashed from my husband's head after the hummers came. He has remodeled our kitchen, installed new appliances, tiled walls; he does complicated four-color silk-screening. He has built an insect-shooter, planning to add butterflies, dragonflies, and bumblebees to his hummingbird portfolio. He's using his mind and wits in ways that he never did before.

Most mystifying is the astonishing fact that Russell's eye hemorrhaging has stopped; there have been no more operations or serious diabetic complications, no more trips to the hospital since he began photographing hummingbirds so many years ago. It's the longest time he has spent out of the hospital in 36 years!

We're keeping our fingers crossed. We do not dismiss lightly the medical realities. Nor do we wish to impart false hope to others. But if Russell's health has not actually improved, at least it *seems* to be no worse. He still sees as well as he did, sometimes I think better. The other day he saw a hummingbird perched in our orange tree.

"Look at him preen!" he exclaimed.

It wasn't the flash of color, the sound of chic-chics, or the whir of wings that he recognized. It was the bird itself.

Often as I wonder at the sunburst explosion of Russell's inner powers beyond seeing, I ask myself how this can be. But who can explain an awakening of spirit and mind? Who knows why or how a new self is born in a man because he suddenly saw a hummingbird?

You can't be suspicious of a tree, or
accuse a bird or a squirrel of subversion
or challenge the ideology of a violet.

HAL BORLAND

LAMPO, THE DOG WHO RODE TRAINS

BY
ELVIO BARLETTANI

It was a warm day in August when I first saw him as he jumped from a freight car at Campiglia Marittima, a busy railway station on Italy's main north-south Rome-Turin line. He seemed an ordinary mutt, medium-sized, with longish white hair and reddish-brown patches. Moments later, in the ticket office where I work, two imploring eyes looked up at me. "Hi!" I said. "What are you doing here?" He knew by my tone of voice that he was welcome, and began to wag his tail and nuzzle my leg.

From that hot day in 1953, he became my shadow. Since he had come into my life so unexpectedly, I decided to call him *Lampo*—"Flash." When the weather was good, he'd lie out on the platforms, enjoying the sun and observing the trains and passengers. But his favorite spot was my office. When I took the train home at night to Piombino, nine miles west of Campiglia, it was an effort to persuade Lampo not to follow me. As the train pulled out, he would tag alongside it for a long way; then, realizing it was futile, he would sadly return to the station.

One night as I sat in the train, I realized Lampo was lying at my feet. He raised his head and gave me a smug look. "How did you ever manage to get on?" I said angrily, pushing him under the seat to keep him out of sight. Luckily it was a short ride, and the conductor didn't notice him.

When we arrived home, my four-year-old daughter, Mirna, ran to greet us. "So this is Lampo," she cried joyfully. At dinner he was our guest of honor. But afterward he began eyeing the door, and at the first opportunity he darted through it and vanished. I did not see him again until the following day at Campiglia. Calm and collected as a ticket-holding passenger, he had taken the train back to his chosen abode.

Lampo quickly learned that my shift ended at 9:00 P.M. He always waited for me on Platform 4. When I was sure the conductor wouldn't see him, I'd signal. He'd climb on board and immediately crawl under the seat, not to emerge until we reached Piombino. He'd visit with us until about 10:30, then trot to the station to catch the last train back at 10:40.

But Lampo did not limit himself to the evening journey. Soon he knew the timetable of all the trains to and from Piombino. In fact, every morning the faithful dog took the 7:20 out from Campiglia, arriving punctually at our house at eight to accompany my daughter to kindergarten. He then caught a train back to Campiglia, only to return to Piombino at 11:30 to accompany Mirna home.

Sometimes he joined us at the beach, apparently guided there by instinct when he didn't find us at home. He loved to swim and roll in the sand. At times, he'd stand and look far out to sea. There was a strange restlessness about him.

During the afternoon, Lampo would doze in the corner of my office until three, then he'd nudge open the door and leave, returning minutes later licking his whiskers contentedly. Once I followed him. He made his way to Platform 1 just as the Turin-Rome express pulled in,

and trotted alongside until he reached the dining car. There he stopped and waited. Imagine my surprise when a cook appeared at the kitchen window and threw him pieces of meat. Lampo gobbled them all up and then returned to my office.

One winter day I saw Lampo eyeing the Rome-Genoa express. Missing him hours later, I suspected that he had boarded the train. I called all the stations on the way to Genoa and told my colleagues to watch for him. That evening, when Mirna asked about the dog, I changed the subject.

The following morning I heard my wife say, "Get down, Lampo, you know you are not allowed up on the chairs." I rushed to the kitchen. "When did he arrive?" I asked.

"At eight, as usual," my wife replied.

After that, it was clear that Lampo had succumbed to the fascination of cross-country train travel. He started with short journeys, then went on to visit nearly all the stations within a range of 200 miles, including the ones on the feeder lines. He even traveled to Rome. As news of his exploits spread, railwaymen amused themselves by fastening outdated tickets around his neck, or railway-pass facsimiles that read: "Free-circulation permit for Lampo, railway dog." But no one could explain why he traveled or how he always found the right train back to Campiglia. As the dog's journeys became increasingly frequent, complicated, and mysterious, we were forced to agree that he was endowed with a sixth sense.

Some officials objected to Lampo's illegal travels. It's not safe to have a loose dog on a train, they said. What if he should bite a passenger? To make matters worse, during one trip Lampo got caught in some automatic doors just as they were closing, and the train had to be stopped. Finally the inevitable happened. "Get rid of the dog," the stationmaster warned me, "or I'll call the dogcatcher."

Back in my office, I talked it over with my colleagues, and we decided to send Lampo off the same way he had come: to put him on a train going as far away as possible.

That evening the conductor of the nonstop train for Naples agreed to transfer him to another fast train bound farther south. The dog would be let off, in open country, far away from any station. We were all present to see him off. From the freight car he looked at us with sad, imploring eyes.

Months went by, and as I worked, my attention was often drawn to the empty corner where Lampo used to sleep. Each evening when I arrived home, Mirna asked, "Has he come back, Daddy?" After a time she no longer asked, and I thought she had forgotten him, until one evening, going by her room, I heard her praying: "Dear Virgin Mary, do protect Lampo. Make sure he is well and finds his way back to us."

The arrival of the first swallows signaling spring cheered everyone a little, but the station wasn't the same. We all felt guilty, even the stationmaster. He would turn and walk away whenever people spoke about the dog.

Then one day one of my colleagues flung open the door shouting, "Come and see!" I hurried out. In front of me stood a very thin ghost, wagging his tail slowly as he looked up at me with two dark, tired eyes. Overcome, I hugged him. "Lampo, dear Lampo!" He licked my face several times. The station echoed with shouts of joy. I wiped away my tears. The stationmaster patted the dog and with ill-concealed emotion said, "Look after him. He's here to stay."

Lampo walked with difficulty. The pads of his feet were swollen and cracked; his ribs protruded from his emaciated body. I took him to a vet.

"Not only has the dog suffered greatly, but he has also caught an intestinal infection," he said. "It's no use."

But the next morning Lampo was on his feet, waiting for me in my office. I ran to fetch a cup of warm milk, which he drank greedily. Perhaps the worst was over. The arrival of the fast train finally set our fears to rest. He pricked up his ears and made his way to the dining car for his usual handout.

Completely recovered, Lampo naturally resumed his travels. No longer hindered, he now roved practically everywhere, getting off one train only to board another. But he did not neglect his duties: punctually every morning he came to our house to accompany Mirna to school. And in the evening he took the train to Piombino with me.

A dog wags its tail with its heart.

MARTIN BUXBAUM

Where had he been all those months? From Naples, a railwayman had taken him east to Bari. The dog had jumped off the train at the station of Barletta—on the Adriatic coast, 425 miles from Campiglia. Later, he was spotted wandering outside the Reggio Calabria station, making a total of 744 miles one way. We shall never know how many miles he covered or how many trains he boarded before he found the right ones to bring him back.

By now, Lampo had become a celebrity. Everyone wanted to hear about his return. The Italian Broadcasting Corp. featured him on a radio program. Television did a film.

One afternoon as Lampo stood on Platform I waiting for his handout from the Turin-Rome dining car, a skinny little old man in a tattered jacket approached, stopped, stared at the dog, and ran toward him. Lampo pricked up his ears; then, wildly wagging his tail, he jumped and placed his front paws on the stranger's knees. "You old brigand!" the man said. "I thought you were dead."

"Do you know this dog?" I asked, walking over.

"Certainly," he replied. "He's the American." He explained how he was a port watchman at Livorno and had seen Lampo come ashore one day from an American ship. The sailors had looked everywhere for him, but finally the ship departed, leaving the dog behind. He stood on the dock for days looking out to sea.

The old man explained that he had taken care of the dog until one day he disappeared. He learned later that when the dog was about to be captured by the dogcatcher, a porter at the Livorno railway station had put him on the freight train that brought him to Campiglia.

I offered the old man a glass of wine and told him of the dog's life at Campiglia. Lampo fell asleep at the old man's feet. "I would like to have him back with me," he said suddenly. "I am alone, and the dog would keep me company."

I helped him get on the train. Lampo followed without hesitation and lay down at his feet. The old man gave me an embarrassed, pleading look. "Let the dog decide," I said. "If he doesn't want to stay, don't worry. He will find his way back by himself."

As the train departed, I returned to my office. Now I understood why, at the beach, Lampo had often gazed out to sea.

Four days later Lampo returned to Campiglia. He seemed sad, and occasionally he would disappear, apparently to visit his friend in Livorno.

Seven summers passed, and Lampo was old now, full of aches and pains. What strength remained he reserved for his trips to Piombino to visit my family. He stopped going to Livorno. The old man had died, I learned later.

With the return of warmer weather, Lampo regained some of his vigor. He even resumed a bit of traveling, which testified to his vitality and his joy of living. But it was only an interlude. Soon, as I boarded the homebound train, I'd look back to see him struggling to get on. Panting, he would give up and look up at me with pleading eyes. I'd extend a hand and help him.

Then on a fine evening in July, just as my train was due to leave, I heard voices and exclamations in the station officials' office. I hurried over. The head signalman, pale, turned to me. "Lampo is dead. He went under a train," he said.

A lump formed in my throat. In a daze, I stared out the window. Finally I walked toward my train, mechanically looking left. In the distance, between engine wheels and rails, I saw a still white form. I didn't want to see him close up; I couldn't face it. Lampo had been killed on his way to wait for me.

"You'd think it was one of us that had been run over," a signalman said to me.

"He *was* one of us," I said, and boarded the train.

My family was waiting for me—the look on my wife's face told me she already knew. "Lampo has left on a long journey," I said, taking Mirna's hand as we walked home.

In March 1962, a life-size statue of this beloved and extraordinary animal was erected at the Campiglia Marittima station. It stands there today, a friend to all travelers.

The dog was created specially for children.

He is the god of frolic.

ISAAC WATTS

WHERE THE SUN SPILLED GOLD

BY
JAROLDEEN EDWARDS

It was a bleak, rainy day, and I had no desire to drive up the winding mountain road to my daughter Carolyn's house. But she had insisted that I come see something at the top of the mountain.

So here I was, reluctantly making the two-hour journey through fog that hung like veils. By the time I saw how thick it was near the summit, I'd gone too far to turn back. *Nothing could be worth this,* I thought as I inched along the perilous highway.

"I'll stay for lunch, but I'm heading back down as soon as the fog lifts," I announced when I arrived.

"But I need you to drive me to the garage to pick up my car," Carolyn said. "Could we at least do that?"

"How far is it?" I asked.

"About three minutes," she said. "I'll drive—I'm used to it."

After ten minutes on the mountain road, I looked at her anxiously. "I thought you said three minutes."

She grinned. "This is a detour."

Turning down a narrow track, we parked the car and got out. We walked along a path that was thick with old pine needles. Huge black-green evergreens towered over us. Gradually the peace and silence of the place began to fill my mind.

Then we turned a corner—and I stopped and gasped in amazement.

From the top of the mountain, sloping for several acres across folds and valleys, were rivers of daffodils in radiant bloom. A profusion of color—from the palest ivory to the deepest lemon to the most vivid salmon—blazed like a carpet before us. It looked as though the sun had tipped over and spilled gold down the mountainside.

At the center cascaded a waterfall of purple hyacinths. Here and there were coral-colored tulips. And as if this bonanza were not enough, western bluebirds frolicked over the heads of the daffodils, their magenta breasts and sapphire wings like a flutter of jewels.

A riot of questions filled my mind. *Who created such beauty? Why? How?*

As we approached the home that stood in the center of the property, we saw a sign: ANSWERS TO THE QUESTIONS I KNOW YOU ARE ASKING.

The first answer was: ONE WOMAN—TWO HANDS, TWO FEET, AND VERY LITTLE BRAIN. The second was: ONE AT A TIME. The third: STARTED IN 1958.

As we drove home, I was so moved by what we had seen I could scarcely speak. "She changed the world," I finally said, "one bulb at a time. She started almost forty years ago, probably just the beginning of an idea, but she kept at it."

The wonder of it would not let me go. "Imagine," I said, "if I'd had a vision and worked at it, just a little bit every day, what might I have accomplished?"

Carolyn looked at me sideways, smiling. "Start tomorrow," she said. "Better yet, start today."

THE CATFISH THAT WALKED

BY
JUNE MELLIES RENO

A waitress hovered nearby as I scanned the menu in a rather good seafood restaurant in New York City. "Catfish?" I asked dubiously.

"Try it," she said. "Tastes like Dover sole—at half the price."

"Okay," I replied. "Bring it on."

As I waited, my mind flashed back to the year 1928, when I was seven years old. I was seated midthwart in a johnboat, a blunt-nosed, flat-bottomed skiff, moored to an elderbush that arched over a quiet swirl of the Mississippi near St. Genevieve, Missouri. My grandmother was perched in the stern, her parasol clutched between her knees, her hands busy with her tatting—those endless little cotton circles and knots. Grandfather was at the prow, lazily netting sunfish for supper.

Quite suddenly, Grandpa bent and peered over the side. Grandpa seldom swore, but now he did: "Golly damn."

"George!" said Grandma.

"Golly damn!" insisted Grandpa. "That's the biggest catfish I ever saw. Must be Ol' Man River himself. I'm going after him."

We looked. Floating a foot beneath the surface was a catfish the size of a mature watermelon. He had a thick, slick gray hide, whiskers drooping from a wide, serene mouth, little horns rising like the quizzical eyebrows of an aging college professor. Yellow eyes.

Nowadays, on modern fish farms, catfish are fed scientifically balanced diets. But 40 years ago this breed was not a company dish. Nor served in fancy restaurants. The catfish's natural food is garbage and offal, scavenged from the river. But Grandma never apologized for putting catfish on her table, albeit disguised in a smother of tomatoes and green peppers. If she heard a complaint, she said, "Never mind what this fish ate. If it didn't kill him, it won't kill you."

The catfish has never been a sportsman's choice. You have to angle for him with stinkbait—Limburger cheese, smelly chicken entrails, or something equally fragrant. And, long considered the most intelligent of freshwater fish, and known to live to a great old age, he will often disdainfully ignore the bait even though you lower it in front of his nose. Once hooked, though, he becomes either fierce or elusive.

Ol' Man River made shrewd use of both those tactics. Grandpa, the day after he issued his challenge, selected a stout handline and began angling from an overhanging bank. He sighted the big old cat—and felt the hook set.

"Got him!" Grandpa hollered, jumping to his feet and heaving taut on the line. "No, you don't," he shouted. "You don't get my line lassoed around the reeds." Then: "Jehosaphat!"

Mother and I ran out the back door and down the steps past Grandma, who was tatting. "It sounds like the head of the household has fallen into the backwater," said Grandma placidly. "Again."

We all reached the bank as Grandpa surfaced. His silver hair dripped pale-brown slime. He shook his fist at the catfish. The creature

was plainly visible as it wriggled across the shallow mud flat that separated the inlet from the mainstream.

"I vow, that cat is walking!" Grandma said.

My mother, who had a way of knowing about such things, said, "There is a species of catfish that uses its pectoral fins to walk as much as half a mile on land."

The fish eased over the bar. With Grandpa's hand-wrought iron hook and a length of twine tangled in his lower jaw, he gave a haughty flip of his tail and submerged.

A feud now ensued that was to last five years. The whole family took part. In the summers, my cousins and I were dispatched each day to patrol the riverbank. Sometimes we saw him, the fishhook still hanging from his mouth. It gave him a contemptuous sneer that plainly said, "I see you two-legged critters. Yours aren't the only brains that got passed around. I know what you're after, and you're not going to get it."

Word spread that our clan had gone a little strange. "They're spending more time fishing than farming!"

One fall, Uncle Hank came and set out after Ol' Man River with an expensive rod and reel designed for Gulf tuna. A county judge and banker, he was our affluent relative. He landed a four-inch bass. But not the big cat.

The earth turned, the fishing went on. We children were growing up, and no longer larked along the river. Grandpa was aging, too. He spent more time dozing in the willow grove than farming or fishing.

Meanwhile, aunts, uncles, and kissin' kin still gathered each August in the pause between tilling and harvest for a family reunion. It was a merry gathering, with gossip paramount among the women, while the men strolled around faulting horses, autos, and real estate.

Uncle Hank, on top of it as ever, arrived in a bright-red La Salle, a handsome golden retriever on the front seat beside him. The auto was promptly put down as unsafe, the dog as incompetent.

Unperturbed, Uncle Hank tossed sticks into the waters of the inlet and hollered, "Fetch!" All agreed that the dog retrieved very well.

I scampered to help lay out the big trencher table with biscuits, honey, potato salad, mounds of squash, eggplant, and green beans. Mother served a succulent ham from the smokehouse. There were pitchers of bock beer, decanters of homemade wine, and fresh, golden milk from our Jersey herd.

Assembled and feasting, we lost track of Uncle Hank's retriever. Suddenly, about 30 feet offshore, there was splashing turmoil. We saw the dog struggling in deep water. As we jumped to our feet, he found bottom. His hindquarters waving, he was hunching backward into the shallows.

Uncle Hank waded out to meet the dog just as he dragged in a very large catfish. Teeth were neatly through the tail. The grounded fish flopped angrily, relaying self-disgust. "Caught by a dog. How humiliating!"

Unmistakably, it was Ol' Man River. He was now nearly five feet in length, and his ID card—Grandpa's rusted fishhook—was still cramped beneath his lower jaw.

As the sun set, a furious family argument took place. *Bury him in the front yard. Raise a monument. Stuff him and hang him over the fireplace.*

Grandma said, "We're going to throw him in the oven. But it's too dark to see to skin him now. Fill the horse trough, and put him in there so he'll keep alive until morning." It was done.

That evening, I washed dishes for more than 50 people. Exhausted, I said good night. But I couldn't sleep. Ol' Man River was captured. The crunch of maturity was suddenly upon me. From longing to grow up, I suddenly didn't want it.

I got out of bed, tiptoed toward the staircase, and bumped into my mother. "Why aren't you in bed?" she said.

"Why aren't you?"

We found Grandma in the kitchen, peering out the back door. "Hear that dratted fish?" she said crossly. "Flopping around, keeping all of us awake. Your grandfather is so restless he's wandering around outside, Lord knows where!"

"The fish wants to live," my mother said gently.

"Please, let's turn him loose," I implored. "He's given us such good sport over the years."

"Your grandfather would never hear of it."

"Doesn't have to. We'll just slip him back into the river."

"How do we move him?" asked Grandma. "He's pretty heavy."

I got an old sheet and a couple of broom handles, and constructed a makeshift stretcher. Gingerly, we lifted the door latch and squinted into the sharp moonlight. Someone moved out of the shadows.

It was Grandpa, with a burlap feed bag over his shoulder. As we watched, he sacked the now groggy fish, heaved him out of the trough, and dragged him toward the riverbank. We scuttled back to bed.

In the morning, we were all surprised to find that the catfish had disappeared. Except Grandpa. "I knew it from the start," he said. "That damn catfish can walk!"

Back in the restaurant, my plate was empty. My reverie had taken longer than I thought. I hope I didn't eat one of Ol' Man River's grandchildren. Probably not. I expect they're as wise and stubborn as their grandpa—and mine.

Summer afternoon—summer afternoon;
to me those have always been the two most
beautiful words in the English language.

HENRY JAMES

CALL OF THE WILD

BY
PENNY PORTER

For wild creatures that roamed our Arizona ranch, life was hard and hunger was constant. Feral dogs lusted after our newborn calves. Frantic raccoons plundered my chicken coop. Coyotes howled their endless distress. But it was the piteous cries of wild cats, solo wanderers of the desert, that tore at my heart. With no place to call home, these castaway descendants of domestic cats reverted to a primal life. And every year when hunger stalked the parched mountains and ranges, many sought refuge on our property.

One cold March morning I was milking my cow while our five domestic barn cats rubbed against my jeans, impatient to be fed. *They don't know what hunger is,* I thought, trying to count the skeletal wild cats cowering behind feed bins. Most were ill. Many were pregnant. Some were hideously scarred, mute evidence of desperate battles for life.

My chore was interrupted when Jaymee, the youngest of our six children, rushed into the barn cupping a snow-white newborn kitten in her hands. Behind its left ear was a copper patch of calico. "All its brothers and sisters are dead!" Jaymee cried.

"I'll bet the great horned owl got them," I said. "You've got to find its mother—it needs to nurse."

"She's dead too!" wailed Jaymee. "What are we going to do, Mama?"

Jaymee had watched us struggle to keep orphaned calves and foals alive. Now she'd found something just the right size for a six-year-old: a precious scrap of life she could hold, love, and take care of by herself. "Without a mama it'll die, won't it?" she asked.

"Yes," I answered. "It'll take a miracle to save it."

We took the kitten inside, wrapped it in a wool mitten, and fed it antibiotic-laced milk from an eyedropper. Then we placed it in a round incubator we used to hatch chicks of rare-breed hens.

"Can I keep the incubator in my room?" Jaymee asked.

I nodded. "But don't tell Daddy about it yet. You know how he feels about cats." Wild cats can have rabies and ringworm, and Bill worried our cattle could become infected. I knew Jaymee would get attached, and worst of all, something told me this cat wouldn't be around for very long. And if she took off, I was sure Jaymee's heart would break. But for now, so much hope shined in my little girl's eyes that I had to help.

Soon afterward Bill—unlit pipe clenched between his teeth—came in for breakfast. "Darn mice chewed holes in nearly every sack of grain in the barn," he said, gulping his coffee. "You'd think our cats"—meaning our pet cats—"could keep them under control. That's why we have 'em. But they have to spend all their time chasing off those wild ones. I've never seen so many wild cats. They're nesting all over the place. Those miserable creatures look sick." I decided that for now I'd keep quiet about Jaymee's kitten.

That night Jaymee and Becky, her nine-year-old sister, fed the tiny kitten, then returned it to the plastic-domed incubator. I heard Becky

whisper to Jaymee, "I counted twenty-two wild cats in the barn this morning! Daddy's having a conniption."

"Does he know we really have twenty-three?" Jaymee asked.

"Not yet."

Nine days later Jaymee showed her father the kitten in the incubator. Bill huffed a little and left the room. The next morning the kitten's eyes opened, and Jaymee named it Miracle.

There could be no other name for this tiny, pink-nosed surprise. My hope was that we could raise Miracle as a domestic cat, a barn cat. But more and more I saw signs that she would never be tied down. Instead of sleeping in her own bed like a domestic cat, Miracle preferred hiding in closets and behind drapes. Other times we found her in Bill's boots or snoozing under beds. The household question became "Where's Miracle?"

At last the morning came when Bill caught Miracle skydiving from the drapes. And when she spiraled up Bill's jeans with claws unsheathed, he decreed that the enclosed back porch would become her new home.

One morning Jaymee was late for breakfast. "Mirry's not on the porch," she said miserably.

"She has to be there somewhere," I said. We searched everywhere, but no kitten.

"I'm going to put food in her bowl anyway," Jaymee said, glancing at her father. "She's just playing a game, you know."

Of course, I thought. *A game wild cats excel at. Hiding!*

For days Miracle's bowl was empty by morning, yet we still couldn't find her. Then we noticed black paw prints from the fireplace to the food and water and back again. "Daddy!" Jaymee squealed. "Mirry's in the chimney! We've got to get her out!"

"I'm not going up there after a cat," Bill grumbled. "She'll come down."

Jaymee turned to her nineteen-year-old brother. "Please, Scott," she begged. Moments later his long arm reached through the partially opened damper. "Got her!" Scott shouted, pulling the coal-black ball of fluff out of the flue.

"Oh, Mirry, you bad girl!" Jaymee exclaimed, then rushed off to clean the kitten up. Unlike most cats, Miracle relished being bathed—and especially liked the blow-dryer.

We offered Miracle marbles, jacks, and fluffy ribbons that domestic cats like to play with, but she was never interested. Instead she waited impatiently for trips outdoors, where she came to life, darting into alfalfa fields or crouching outside my chicken coop, trembling with desire at the sight of 200 chicks. "Look, how cute! She wants to play with them!" Jaymee said.

Play? A twitching tail? Tiny claws extending and retracting? I wasn't so sure. I'd read that the skill to kill must be taught by a cat's mother. But I couldn't help wondering if such a trait might come more naturally to Miracle. Soon after, at the age of seven months, the nighttime yowling began. Was it her call of the wild?

"She sees things in the dark that we can't see," Jaymee said at breakfast. "Secrets and . . ."

". . . tomcats!" Bill added. He was stiff-necked and grouchy from sleeping with his head under the pillow, trying to block out Miracle's nocturnal wailing. "Darn cat," he muttered.

One evening Bill came in for dinner with a handful of rattlesnake rattles. "We found a nest of more than fifty of the critters over at Cowan's ranch," he said. He selected the biggest and shook it. Instantly Miracle's nose pushed against the kitchen window. Her back arched, her flinty eyes sparked. We gave her a rattle to play with, and suddenly it was clicking and skittering across the floor like a hockey puck, Miracle in fierce pursuit. Our little cat honed her feline skills on this new toy—and prey.

One day I discovered a round sore on Miracle's forehead. At first I suspected she'd been hurt until blisters and circles erupted on Jaymee's face and neck as well.

"Ringworm," said the vet after examining both cat and child under a diagnostic blue light. There the pair glittered like glowworms on a summer night. After administering the treatment for Jaymee and Miracle, the vet said, "And warn Bill to watch those bulls. This strain could prove contagious."

Nature breaks through the eyes of a cat.

IRISH PROVERB

That night Bill came in for supper, beat. "Two of the show bulls have ringworm," he said.

Inwardly I cringed. I thought of the quarantine, the cost of antibiotics and lime sulfur dips for animals weighing close to 2000 pounds. I wanted to tell Bill about Miracle, but Jaymee beat me to it.

"Oh, Daddy!" she said. "Think how beautiful the bulls would look under the blue light! Mirry and I sparkled like angels!" Bill didn't get angry, as I'd expected. Even he couldn't help grinning at Jaymee's description.

One evening a few weeks later, Miracle didn't come when we called. Then the phone rang. "Does your little girl have a white cat?" asked a hay buyer who'd picked up a ton of alfalfa just before noon. He lived 60 miles away.

"Yes," I said.

"I reckon it likes to ride in trucks," he continued. "Didn't know it was there till I got home."

A muscle flicked in Bill's jaw as he reached for his hat. Moments later he and Jaymee disappeared into the darkness for the 120-mile round-trip to fetch her cat.

Before long, Miracle became a seasoned wanderer. Although cars and trucks were a favorite mode of travel, she vanished more often on foot and was gone for days, even weeks at a time.

On Miracle's first birthday I heard Scott yell from a horse corral. "Miracle! Get outta there!" And in the next breath, "Dad! Rattler!"

Bill grabbed a shovel from the pickup, and I dashed for the antivenin kit. The diamondback had struck a mare between the nostrils. The horse was staggering, pawing the ground, her eyes white-rimmed with panic. In minutes her head began to swell. She couldn't breathe.

Quickly Bill inserted a breathing tube and administered the antidote. We prayed the crisis would pass. Then Scott said to his father, "If it hadn't been for Miracle, that flash of white, I wouldn't have seen this happen. The cat was going bonkers, Dad, leaping around and jumping at those rattles." He looked at me. "Mom, I think the snake got Miracle too."

When we found the little cat, she lay motionless—eyes sealed, her head swollen. The bottle of antivenin serum was empty. "I'll try some cortisone," Bill said. "It's all we've got."

I laid the lifeless ball of fluff gently in her box. Jaymee knelt beside her kitten, murmuring, "You'll be okay, sweetheart." After two days in a coma, Miracle started to improve. We vowed we'd never let her outside again. But as her strength returned, so did her nomadic ways.

Miracle was 2½ when she disappeared for the last time. We missed her terribly. Even Bill, in his own private way.

Over the next few years Jaymee would come to love many cats, but the memory of Miracle always remained closest to her heart. Often, before bedtime, she would come with me when I checked on the chickens or a newborn foal. With her flashlight Jaymee would light up empty mangers and passageways between bales of hay. "Better be careful," I'd remind her. Jaymee's answer was always the same: "I *am,* Mama. But I can't stop looking for Miracle."

One evening three years later, Bill came in the back door, his eyes bright with mischief. "Jaymee!" he called. "Come outside a minute!" We all followed.

Camouflaged against the weathered metal barn roof crouched a battered little cat. Its dusty fur was puckered with scars, its right ear pasted to its skull. But the left ear, though ripped and torn, betrayed a trace of calico.

"Mirry!" Jaymee whispered, her face glowing with excitement.

All of us shared Jaymee's joy, but I also felt concern because I was sure this was no longer the "Mirry" she'd loved years before. This was a battle-hardened wild cat. In her world there could be no room for memories of the little girl who'd held her and bathed her and cherished her quirky little ways. Jaymee had been shattered when Miracle disappeared for those three years. Would she be hurt even worse now when Miracle failed to recognize her?

Meanwhile, spellbound, we all watched as Miracle's eyes fixed on a small bird nearby. "No, Mirry!" Jaymee screamed.

The cat hesitated. Then, shifting her gaze toward Jaymee's familiar voice, she eased down and leapt into Jaymee's outstretched arms. "I knew you'd come back!" Jaymee said. "I knew it!"

Except for occasional two-day trips, Miracle roamed no more. She ate cat food, left mice on the back doorstep, and seemed to settle down to domestic cat life—until the morning Bill found her on the seat of his tractor. Her rugged little heart had simply stopped. She was seven years old. "At least Mirry died at home," Jaymee said quietly. "She died with her family."

Jaymee and all of us had learned a lesson that would stay with us forever: even in the strangest of animal cultures, a child's love *can* overcome the ultimate call of the wild.

What is man without the beasts? If all the beasts were gone, man would die from a great loneliness of spirit. For whatever happens to the beasts, soon happens to man. All things are connected.

CHIEF SEATTLE

STRANGE ENCOUNTER WITH A BLUE JAY

BY
THOMZA ZIMMERMAN

I don't expect anyone to put credence in the story I am about to tell. Then why do I write it? I'm not quite sure. Maybe because a remembered experience is more easily put aside for all time after it is written down. Maybe because I walked through the yard this morning and picked up a blue jay's feather.

The story has to do with a jaybird that lived with us for more than two years. We called him Pesty.

But not at first. At first he was just the unfortunate ball of gray fluff that fell from the nest in the maple tree. I didn't relish the thought of the hapless creature being devoured by a passing cat, so I took him in.

As I put him into a box lined with toweling, I hoped he would not be too uncomfortable during his few remaining hours of life. My husband, Lyman, came in from his work in the fields, peered into the box, and grinned. Without knowing it, we had been taken over by a jaybird.

The name Pesty came as he grew older, when he began to catch bugs and happily store them away in my freshly done hair, lift the blossoms from a bouquet and take a bath in the bowl, and object in no uncertain terms when a guest unwittingly sat in Lyman's chair.

But this is not what makes the story so different or so strange. The unbelievable part came later. More than a year after Pesty was gone.

From the day Lyman brought a fat earthworm from the garden to supplement Pesty's diet of boiled egg yolks and baked pie crust, Pesty became Lyman's bird. He perched on the arm of his chair and waited, with no sign of impatience or boredom, while Lyman read the paper. If Lyman napped, Pesty sat quietly on his shoulder. Though Pesty didn't like being fondled ("I'll make the advances," his manner quickly told you), at bedtime Lyman would pick him up from wherever he happened to be—the mantel, the top of a curtain, the back of a chair—and hold him a moment against his cheek, where Pesty actually snuggled. Then Lyman carried him to his nighttime perch, a bathroom towel bar.

When daylight edged its way through the east windows, I would feel a soft touch on my pillow and then a bobby pin being slipped gently from my hair. Pesty knew I got up first to start breakfast. It was time.

Although his food and water were always in the kitchen window, Pesty preferred eating at the table. "He thinks he's people," our neighbor would say. And Pesty's favorite meal, like most country people's, was breakfast. He drank coffee from a butter-pat-size saucer, and ate scrambled eggs—with butter, thank you. When he was finished, he hopped to Lyman's shoulder and waited politely until we were through too.

Like a boy following in the footsteps of his father, Pesty took up smoking. In one quick movement he could have a cigarette from the pocket in Lyman's shirt. At first, we thought it was clever and enjoyed telling people about it. But when he made attempts to light his cigarette, a scorched rug resulted. After that, the matches were kept in a drawer.

Pesty's level of intelligence never ceased to amaze us. He learned the sound of Lyman's tractor and the car. When he heard either of them coming he went quickly to the door to welcome Lyman home.

Pesty chose his own friends, and he preferred men. When Lyman had company over to play cards, Pesty sat in on the game from the safety of Lyman's shoulder. The cards fascinated him, and with his dexterity he had to be watched. He could take a card quickly and make off with it. This brought about a chase and sometimes a scolding from Lyman, but it heightened the evening's fun.

We never confined our bird to the house. We wanted him to know the outdoors and expected that someday he would join his kind. But the yard birds resented him intensely, and he usually preferred to stay in the house.

There was a day, however, when he chose to stay outdoors. It was a balmy, summer-scented morning, and Lyman and I were going to join friends for an all-day picnic. When we were ready to go, Pesty was outside. We tried to bring him in, but he wasn't ready.

Pesty seemed not to have an adequate supply of oil in his feathers. After a bath he could never fly, and walked around like a decrepit little old man until he was dry again. For this reason Lyman scanned the sky. "There's no sign of rain," he concluded, and we left. Before we returned there was a severe downpour.

Lyman called and looked and hunted for days, but we never found Pesty.

The summer ended, the harvest was in, we made ready for winter. In due time the snows melted, the crocus came up, spring passed, and again it was summer. The wild rose was blooming in old fence rows; the smell of honeysuckle was heavy on the morning air.

I was busy in the kitchen when I heard the birds making a great commotion. The raucous cries of the blue jays had brought them all: the robins and cardinals, the mockingbird and wrens, the brown thrasher and the orioles. Even the indigo bunting came from the raspberry border, and I went too. They were gathered over and around the garage where a lone blue jay was sitting on a crosspiece above the door. The hostility of the other birds told me he was a stranger.

With my arrival the yard birds settled down and went back to their various concerns, but the new bird remained. His shorter tail marked him as a young bird, hatched just that spring. His eyes were bright, his beak strong and straight. A bird analyst would have called him a fine, healthy specimen.

The young blue jay looked at me with a show of interest that held no fear. *He may be hungry,* I thought, and brought a cookie. When I offered it, he bent down and nibbled.

Rabbits live and frolic at random in our garden. Squirrels feed in our corncrib and then play on the roof. In winter, birds eat from feeders with only a windowpane between them and us. There is a joy in being accepted and trusted by a creature of the wild. I knew that joy now, but overriding it was the knowledge that the young jay's behavior was anything but normal. There was something here I didn't understand.

I went around the house and sat on the patio. The bird came and sat on the arm of a chair close by. Later, when I went inside, the bird came with me. He went immediately to the window over the kitchen sink where Pesty used to sit and was there when Lyman came in for lunch.

Lyman stopped halfway across the kitchen and looked at the bird in the window, then turned and looked at me, with his eyes wide and full of questions. I told him what little I could.

When we sat down to eat, the strange bird came and perched on the back of a chair at the table. After a few seconds he hopped up onto Lyman's shoulder. At this, Lyman stiffened visibly, and I thought his face paled. After another minute or two, the bird went back to the window.

The meal ended sooner than it should have. Dessert was refused. Lyman got up and without a glance toward the window started back to work. The bird followed him to the back porch, sat in the window, and watched him go.

I cleared the table, left the dishes in the sink, and went outside. *I'll go for a walk,* I thought. *I'll go to the pasture fence and see if berries are ripening.*

I walked through the pasture but forgot to look for berries. When I came back to the house, the blue jay was still in the back-porch window. He was dead.

I held the small, limp form in my hand, and tears flowed down my cheeks. A flood of questions crowded my mind. Questions . . . without answers.

God made all flying things

Eagle and albatross,

With tapered body and spread of

outstretched wings

To hang against the sunset like a cross.

ALFRED BARRETT

FOX IN THE KITCHEN

BY
AVRIL JOHANNES

When my daughter, Jan, was twelve, our family got devastating news. Jan had a malignant growth that would require a leg amputation. She would have to undergo surgery and long months of rehabilitation.

As any mother would, I worried about my young daughter's spirits. Then one night in the hospital, when sleep evaded her, Jan surprised me by asking, "Mom, remember Vicky?"

Our family lived on a farm along an old logging road near Fairbanks, Alaska. Wildlife abounded in the quiet countryside. One winter night while out walking, my husband, Joe, and I heard a distant cry.

A young fox, the color of autumn maples against the snow, was twisting in an illegal trap. Arching her back to spring into the air, she smashed back to the ground and collapsed.

"Look at that leg," Joe said. "It's destroyed."

Removing his jacket, he gently placed it over the animal. I released her torn leg from the trap, expecting her to lunge to bite me. But under

Joe's coat she did not struggle. Her yellow eyes, bright with pain and fear, stared at us unflinchingly. On the way home we named the little vixen Vicky.

As a veterinary assistant with a background in animal husbandry, I was qualified to rehabilitate injured wildlife for the state of Alaska. When we brought Vicky into the kitchen, she was watched by two owls with frozen feet, hanging in slings inside their cages. A bald eagle with a broken wing clung to the back of the couch, staring. A caged mink we'd found almost frozen to death stuck its nose through the wire and hissed, while our family cat, hair on end, eyed the newcomer warily.

Joe sat at the table gripping Vicky's head securely while I prepared to fix her leg. Our three children gathered around. "Try not to hurt her," whispered seven-year-old Jan, her blond head bent close to the delicate little fox.

Using cotton balls soaked with ether, Joe administered anesthetic. As soon as Vicky was out, I cleaned and disinfected her wound. With tweezers I removed splinters of bone, then scissored away the surrounding fur to expose the shattered bones.

There were four breaks in all. I matched the bones as closely as possible while Joe monitored Vicky's heartbeat. Finally, tying the bones in place with suture, I sewed the skin together, bandaged the entire leg, then strapped on a splint.

Hours after surgery Vicky's eyes fluttered open. She raised her head to look around, but made no move to stand. I draped a blanket over her cage for privacy and left her door ajar.

The next morning Vicky lay on her side breathing evenly. To my astonishment her head rested on a pink, fluffy rug she'd managed to pull into her cage from the living room sometime during the night.

Two mornings later, though, something was very wrong. During the night Vicky had tried to chew off the splint. Now she was trapped by a

shaft of broken bone caught on a bar at the bottom of her cage. The tattered, infected limb was beyond repair. There was no choice—later that day I amputated Vicky's leg.

Long, anxious hours passed before the little fox stirred. I squeezed cold water from a washcloth into her mouth. Joe and I took turns staying close to her the remainder of that day and all through the night. Jan and her brothers, Mark and Scott, only left her side long enough to eat and run to the bathroom.

Within days, however, Vicky began to eat, lap water, and be more alert. I noticed her staring into the living room. Finally it dawned on me what she wanted: the pink rug, which I'd removed from her cage to wash. When I moved it closer, Vicky stuck her face through the bars and pulled it in with her.

We decided to open the cage door again and give her the run of the house. Vicky stood, lost her balance, fell, and tried again. "Oh, Mom," Jan whispered. "She's so brave, and she keeps trying." My own heart ached.

After a few more attempts Vicky managed to stand. From the safety of her cage, she gazed about the room but showed no desire to walk. But late that night I awoke to hear her soft pads cross our bedroom floor. A cool nose brushed against my hand. Then I heard her moving down the hall to the children's rooms.

Soon it seemed that the cage had become her den, the place she returned to for security. She groomed herself there and buried food under her pink rug. No doubt about it, she considered the rug hers. Sometimes she'd take it to sleep with behind the fireplace grate. All we would see was a glimpse of pink.

Vicky now moved about freely, scurrying away if we got too close. Stalking her favorite toy, an old glove, she'd pounce, throw it in the air, and catch it. Then one night I watched fascinated as she padded to the door, stood with her nose to the crack, and sniffed the outside air.

More than seven weeks had slipped by. With breeding season only months away, Vicky needed her freedom to find a new mate and a new den. But before she could be released back into the wild, Joe and I had to know if she could kill prey for herself.

One night Joe released a sacrificial chicken in the kitchen. Vicky didn't make a move. Disappointed, I went to bed. But in the morning Vicky lay in her cage, the partially eaten chicken forming a mound beneath her pink rug.

Almost daily now her restlessness increased. At night she paced the house and looked out the window. In the light of day, fox, ermine, and hare tracks told us what she'd seen.

I had no more excuses. Hadn't I told our children that wild animals should never be considered pets? Though I wanted her to live the life she was born for, I hated the idea of giving her up.

Finally we decided Vicky should go. Dreading the moment, I slowly opened the door, fully expecting her to rush out and vanish. Instead, Vicky stood in the doorway, then went back to her cage and curled up on her rug. "See, Mom," said our son Scott. "She doesn't want to go."

The next evening I opened the door again. Vicky rushed to look. She smelled the night air, reading all it carried. Again she returned to her cage.

Five nights later our fox finally ventured out and disappeared into the trees. Torn by happiness and sadness, Joe and I carried her cage outside in case she returned during the night. Jan and her brothers followed with Vicky's pink rug, her favorite glove and bones, and some food scraps.

Eagerly the next morning we checked the cage. Some of the scraps had been eaten. The rest were buried under her rug. In the snow were Vicky's distinctive three paw prints.

For three weeks Vicky returned every night to eat an egg we'd left for her. One by one she took away the glove and bones. Then one day we found a freshly killed grouse buried in her cage. Jan turned to me and said, "She's going to make it, Mom."

The following night Vicky took away her pink rug. Though we knew she was nearby, this was the last time she would return to her cage.

In June we had to move. The day we left, Vicky sat on a berm watching us. She looked healthy but shaggy in her summer coat.

"Vicky," I said, stopping my car for a final good-bye, "look after yourself." She yapped twice, the only time I ever heard her bark, then scampered off to the life she was designed to live.

Jan and I talked about Vicky for a long time that night in the hospital. Her blue eyes floated in unspilled tears. "You know, Mom," she said, "I won't let anything stop me from doing the things I want to do in life."

My heart quivered. As Jan had once said of Vicky, I found myself thinking of my brave daughter: she's going to make it. And so she has. Today Jan is a wife and full-time mother of two small boys.

As for Vicky, I like to think she found a partner and raised young. Many times I've pictured her unique tracks in the snow. And many times I've wondered if her coming was meant to be, to show us about dealing with life's hardships and joys.

In my heart, I know the answer.

I think I could turn and live with

animals, they're so placid

and self-contained,

I stand and look at them long and long.

WALT WHITMAN

INDIANS DON'T CRY

BY
MICKEY ALLEN

I told them when I signed up as assistant leader that I knew next to nothing about camping and even less about Campfire Girls. Unfortunately, no one batted an eye. That is how I became involved in what follows.

Throughout the school year, a very competent Mrs. Walker kept the Campfire meetings zinging along. All I did was help with the scissors and tape. As summer approached, the girls began talking about camp. Mrs. Walker would be unable to take them. In an unguarded moment, I said I would. "Yea! Hurray for Mrs. Allen," etc.

The yellow bus picked up our scruffy little group at the ungodly hour of 7:30 A.M. As we bounced along, I noticed that the little girl next to me looked pale. "I think I'm going to throw up," she said.

I reached into my purse for a tissue. She was right; she did throw up. Right into my purse.

After an endless 45-minute ride we arrived at an open field with a log cabin and numerous totem poles. A large sergeant-type woman raised her hand, instantly silenced the screaming throng of girls, and announced matter-of-factly, "Your tarps have been folded. Be sure to floor your camps. There have been sightings of poison oak in sections 422, 668, and 669. You will be glad to hear that the rattlesnakes have been completely done away with by the bull snakes. Please do not harm the bull snakes; we now have a population of fourteen. Pick up your supplies and hurry to the powwow."

I hadn't understood half of what she said; but what I had understood scared me to death. Now I know why they bring you on a bus. So you can't leave.

I followed the other mothers (hereinafter called Squaws) to a room marked supplies. I was handed a large, dirty bundle. I dragged this treasure to the powwow in back of the log cabin. The Sergeant was spouting off rules, duties, and latrine locations. Then she dropped the crushing blow: Squaws would not keep their own girls. I was about to venture into the snake-infested wilderness with 12 strangers.

There they stood. Twelve already unbelievably dirty, blue-jeaned, ponytailed, besneakered, nine-year-old Indians.

"Now what?" I said with all the confidence I could muster.

"Now we find our campsite and set up the tarp," said one bright-eyed veteran.

I felt a little uneasiness, but no real panic. "Okay. How about right here next to the lodge?" I suggested.

Laughter. "You *are* funny, Miss Mickey."

I didn't think so.

They led me over a trail that disappeared into wilderness. After traveling for untold miles, they came upon a rotting fallen tree. This, I was told, was a perfect site. Who was I to argue? Besides, I was weak from dragging that tarp thing.

While the 12 little Indians frightened off all of the wildlife within earshot, I tried to figure out what a tarp was. I worked on the knot in the stupid rope until I thought I'd scream.

"Need some help?" said a voice from behind. There stood an angelic child with two blond pigtails.

"Just fixing the tarp," I lied.

In nothing short of a flash she had untied the bundle.

In case you don't know what a tarp is, it is a piece of somebody's old tent that has been thrown away. Our piece was a trapezoid. Inside it were an old shower curtain, a lard can containing a hammer, an axe, an iron skillet, a box of matches, two packages of flower seeds, a can of tick spray, a box of 400 bandages, and, God forbid, a snake-bite kit. I stood looking helplessly at the pile of junk.

"My name is Susie," said my little rescuer.

"Okay, Susie, do you know what to do with this stuff?" I said.

"Well, last year Miss Alice made a three-sided tent out of the tarp, and we built a fence, and we planted . . ."

I had never met Miss Alice, but I hated her instantly.

We wandered around for an hour spying on the other campsites, trying to get the general drift of what to do. The other Squaws had worked wonders. Their camp sported neat tarp shelters, tables, gently burning fires, rope swings.

By the end of the day, our domain sported a funny-looking tarp that hung from one corner by a short rope looped over the top branch of our rotting tree. The other side was held by a rubber band wrapped around a skinny sapling. The front flap was secured by adhesive tape to two long sticks stuck about one inch into the hard ground. We had the largest anthill in the entire camp and a weird hole that the girls convinced me was a snake hole. Our new home. The girls loved it.

By the third day we had taken on the name Blackfoot for our tribe, and I had the dubious title of Fearless Leader. We had had serious discussions such as: When you are out in the wilderness and don't have a tissue, what does a lady do with the remains after she has picked her nose? You may not think this is a very serious problem. But when you are nine years old and in camp it can be very pertinent.

One day when I was hot and cranky, the tarp flap fell (again). I was refixing it while White Cloud, the only black girl in the tribe, stood watching. For no reason at all, she looked me in the eye and said, "I love you, even if you *are* white."

For a moment I forgot about the terrible mosquito-bite itch inside my bra and my sore feet and my sunburn. What could I say? What *should* I say? As I looked into her eyes, I felt my own brimming over.

"Indians don't cry," she scolded.

The last day finally arrived. We broke camp early and trudged back to the big meeting of the tribes by the flagpole. It was 103 degrees that day. We sat Indian-fashion around a huge bonfire. A slightly potbellied Mr. Mack began speaking: "All of us will be taking home fond memories of our beloved camp . . ."

Now I'm not much of one for speeches, so I busied myself trying to scratch the place under my bra and looking at my watch. At four o'clock, the bus would take me home to my indoor plumbing and a nice hot bath.

I was slightly aware of people watching me. I glanced around. My girls were beaming at me. I decided I had better pay attention. ". . . Blackfoot tribe," he was saying. "This is the first time in the camp's history that one tribe has won all three awards.

"The Best Camper goes to Running Deer, Susie." Blond, pigtailed Susie entered the circle to receive her award. "Running Deer saved the camp from burning to the ground by shoveling dirt on a fire in Number Three rest station. Thank you, Running Deer, for your quick thinking.

"The Kindness to Animals award goes to White Cloud, Julie." Proudly, White Cloud entered the circle. "White Cloud found a bull snake badly wounded. She cared for him and brought him food until he was able to hunt for himself.

"Every day as I walked through the camp," Mr. Mack went on, "I inspected the neat campsites with their trim shelters and craft displays and equipment carefully stored. Our campsites looked like a magazine advertisement. That is, until I came upon one particular camp."

Ho, boy, here it comes, I thought.

"This camp had a shaky, lopsided shelter, a sign that read *See the Snake Hole—One Marshmallow,* and another that read *Give Your Unwanted Bugs to Help a Hungry Snake.* The supplies were in confusion, the cooking pit was full of water. At other camps, Indians followed a set routine of crafts and games while Squaws prepared lunch. Not at the Snake Hole."

Nature is the art of God.

DANTE

Go ahead, Jabbermouth, tell everything you know, I thought quietly.

"Here the Squaw and her Indians spent most of the morning trying to light a fire and otherwise survive in the wild. While at first glance this may have looked like an exercise in futility, closer observation proved that the whole group of Indians was totally involved. It was *their* camp. Everything had been learned the hard way—firsthand. The Blackfoot tribe may leave with no more Indian lore than they came with, but they leave with something much more precious: the knowledge of teamwork and personal accomplishment. Fearless Leader, enter the circle and receive your award."

As I stood between Running Deer and White Cloud, I could barely swallow my tears back into my eyes.

When the meeting was over, my little Indians came to me for a last hug. I think they were concerned about who would watch out for me now. When I came to White Cloud, I noticed tear streaks running down her beautiful brown face. "Indians don't cry," I said.

"I'm not an Indian anymore," she said. "I'm just a little girl." Funny how I hadn't thought of that in the last few days.

There should have been 12 more awards given that day. Loyalty awards. They hadn't given me away once. We all acted as if the whole week had gone Exactly as Planned.

There is nothing like walking to get the feel of a country. A fine landscape is like a piece of music; it must be taken at the right tempo. Even a bicycle goes too fast.

PAUL SCOTT MOWRER

"WHERE THERE IS LOVE"

BY
ALETHA JANE LINDSTROM

We got him with the other animals when we bought the farm. Not that we wanted the black, shaggy mongrel. We had our hearts set on a collie—a pup we could train for the farm and as a companion for five-year-old Tim. But when the former owners failed to return for their dog, we resigned ourselves to keeping him. Temporarily, we thought.

"If we ignore him, maybe he'll just take off," I said to Carl, my schoolteacher husband. He didn't. In fact, the big beast apparently considered the farm *his* responsibility. Each dawn, he inspected the animals and the farm buildings. Then he made a complete circuit of the entire 80 acres. That finished, he bounded across the sloping fields to slip beneath the fence for a visit with old Mr. Jolliff, who lived near a brook at the farm's edge.

The big dog—we learned from Mr. Jolliff that his name was Inky—was pensive and aloof those first weeks. Grieving for his former master, Inky asked no affection, and we offered none. Except Tim, who sat by the hour on the back steps, talking softly to the unresponsive animal. Then, one morning, Inky crept close and laid his head in the boy's lap. And before we knew it, he had become Tim's second shadow.

All that summer the boy and the dog romped through fields and roamed the woods, discovering fox dens and groundhog burrows. Each day, they brought back treasures to share. "Mom, we're home!" Tim would shout, holding the screen door wide for Inky. "Come see what we've got!" He'd dig deep in his jeans and spread the contents on the kitchen table: a pheasant's feather; wilted buttercups with petals like wet paint; stones from the brook that magically regained their colors when he licked them.

September arrived all too soon, bringing with it school for Carl and Tim, and lonely days for Inky and me. Previously, I'd paid little attention to the dog. Now he went with me to the mailbox, to the chicken coop, and down the lane when I visited Mr. Jolliff.

"Why didn't they come back for Inky?" I asked Mr. Jolliff one afternoon.

"And shut him up in a city apartment?" Mr. Jolliff replied. "Inky's a farm dog; he'd die in the city. Besides, you're lucky to have him."

Lucky? I thought ruefully of holes dug in the lawn, of freshly washed sheets ripped from the clothesline. I thought, too, of litter dumped on the back porch: old bones, discarded boots, long-dead rodents. And beer cans! Each morning, on his way home from Mr. Jolliff's, Inky retrieved one can from the roadside and placed it neatly on the doorstep. He was noisy, too, challenging each truck and tractor on the road with loud barks that brought me running.

Still, I had to admit that Inky was a good farm dog. We learned this in early spring when his insistent barking alerted us to a ewe, about to lamb, lying on her broad back in a furrow, unable to rise. Without Inky's warning she'd have died. And he had an uncanny way of knowing when roving dogs threatened the flock, or when a sheep went astray.

One morning, instead of a beer can, Inky placed a starving gray kitten on the doorstep. He hovered anxiously while the fluffy mite lapped her fill of warm milk. Then he carried her to his blanket in the barn, licked her thoroughly, and settled down beside her while she slept. From that day on she shared his bed.

But Inky's deepest affection was reserved for Tim. Each afternoon when the school bus lumbered down the road, Inky ran joyously to meet it. For Inky—and for Tim—this was the high point of the day.

One mid-October day when I had been in town, Tim rode home with me after school. He was instantly alarmed when Inky wasn't waiting for us by the driveway.

"Don't worry, Tim," I said. "Inky always expects you on the bus, and we're early. Maybe he's back by the woods."

Tim ran down the lane, calling and calling. While I waited for him to return, I looked around the yard. Its emptiness was eerie.

Suddenly I, too, was alarmed. With Tim close behind me, I ran down to the barn. We pushed the heavy doors apart and searched the dim coolness. Nothing. Then, as we were about to leave, a faint whimper came from the far corner of a horse stall. There we found him, swaying slightly on three legs, his pain-dulled eyes pleading for help. Even in the half-light I could see that one back leg hung limp, the bone partially severed. With a little moan, Tim ran to Inky and buried his face in the dog's neck.

By the time the vet arrived, Carl was home. We placed the dog on his blanket and gently lifted him onto the pet ambulance. Inky whimpered, and Tim started to cry.

"Don't worry, son," the vet said. "He's got a good chance." But his eyes told a different story.

It was Tim's bedtime, so I took him upstairs and heard his prayers. He finished and looked up. "Will Inky be home tomorrow?"

"Not tomorrow, Tim. He's hurt pretty bad."

"You tell me that doctors make people well. Doesn't that mean dogs, too?"

I looked out across the fields flooded with amber light. How do you tell a little boy that his dog must either die, or be a cripple? "Yes, Tim," I said at last. "I guess that means dogs, too." I tucked in his blanket and went downstairs.

Carl had finished chores and was getting ready for a meeting at school. I tossed a sweater over my shoulders. "I'm going down to Mr. Jolliff's," I said. "Maybe he'll know what happened."

I found the old man sitting at his kitchen table in the fading light. He drew up another chair and poured coffee. "Tim in bed?" he asked. "I miss him now he's in school. Thank goodness Inky still comes to see me. Though come to think of it, he didn't show up this morning. I sort of worried about him."

Somehow I couldn't talk about the dog. Instead, I asked, "Do you know if anyone was cutting weeds around here today?"

"Seems to me I heard a tractor down along the brook this morning," Mr. Jolliff replied. "Why?" He looked at me. "Did something happen to Inky?"

"Yes," I said, and the words were tight in my throat. "His back leg's nearly cut off. The vet came for him . . ." I wanted to say more, but couldn't. "It's growing dark," I finally murmured. "I'd better be getting home."

Mr. Jolliff followed me into the yard. "About Inky," he said hesitantly, "if he lives, I'd give him a chance. He'll still have you folks and Tim, the farm and the animals. Everything he loves. Life's pretty precious . . . especially where there's love."

"Yes," I said, "but if he loses a leg, will love make up for being a cripple?"

He said something I didn't catch. But when I turned to him, he'd removed his glasses and was rubbing the back of his stiff old hand across his eyes.

By the time I reached our yard the sun was gone, leaving the world to the magic of cool, thin silver and shadow. I walked down by the barn and stood with my arms on the top fence rail. Beyond the lane the horses were moving toward the woods, grazing as they went. I watched until they vanished like phantoms in the moonlit mist brimming the meadow. Then I dropped my head to my arms and let the tears come.

I cried because Inky had been so gentle with the animals, and because he loved Tim so much, and Tim loved him. But mostly I cried because I hadn't really wanted him; not until now, when this terrible thing had happened. Why do we so seldom know how much we love something until we are faced with its loss?

The day, water, sun, moon, night—I do not have to purchase these things with money.

PLAUTUS

Inky's paw couldn't be saved. Too vividly, I recalled how Inky had raced across fields and meadows, swift and free as a cloud shadow. I listened skeptically as the vet tried to reassure us: "He's young and strong. He'll get along on three legs."

Tim took the news with surprising calmness. "It's all right," he said. "Just so Inky comes home."

"But those long jaunts the two of you take may tire him now," I cautioned.

"He's always waited for me. I'll wait for him. Besides, we're never in much of a hurry."

The vet called a few days later. "You'd better come for your dog. He's homesick." I went immediately, and was shocked at the change in Inky. The light was gone from his eyes. His tail hung limp and tattered, and the stump of his leg was swathed in a stained bandage. He hobbled over and pressed wearily against my leg. A shudder went through the hot, thin body and he sighed—a long, deep sigh filled with all the misery and loneliness of the past few days.

At the farm, I helped Inky from the car. The gray kitten came tumbling through the leaves, but Inky seemed unaware of her. He looked first to the sheep, grazing in the pasture; then, beyond the fields of green winter wheat, to the autumn woods where the horses, dappled with sunlight, moved among the trees. My heart ached as I realized how great must have been his longing for this place. At last, he limped to the barn and slipped between the heavy doors.

While his wound healed, Inky stayed in the barn, coming out only in the evenings. When the low sun slanted across the fields and the horses came up for water, we'd see him standing by the trough. After the horses returned to pasture, he disappeared into the barn.

Throughout those days the sick feeling never left me. *You are a coward to let him live,* I told myself. *Afraid of hurting yourself, of hurting Tim.* But in my heart I wasn't sure. We so seldom know the real reasons for the things we do, or fail to do.

About a week after bringing Inky home, I was in the yard raking leaves. When I'd finished under the maple, I sat on the steps to rest. It was a perfect Indian summer day; our country road was a tunnel of gold, and sumac ran like a low flame along the south pasture. Reluctantly, I reached for the rake.

Then, with a flurry of leaves, Inky was beside me. I knelt and stroked the fur so smooth and shiny again. He moved, and I was achingly aware of the useless limb. "I'm so sorry, Inky," I said, putting my arms around his neck and pressing my head against his.

Sitting awkwardly, he placed his paw on my knee and looked up at me with soft, intelligent eyes. Then he pricked his ears and turned to listen. In an instant, he was off to meet the school bus. He ran with an ungainly, one-sided lope—but he ran with joy.

Tim jumped from the high step and caught the dog in his arms. "Oh, Inky! Inky!" he cried. Inky licked Tim's face and twisted and squirmed with delight. They remained there for a time, oblivious to anything but the ecstasy of being together again.

Watching them, I knew we'd been right to let the dog live. Most of us, God's creatures, are maimed to some extent either physically or emotionally, yet few of us want to die. What was it Mr. Jolliff had said?

"Life's pretty precious . . . especially where there's love."

There is no psychiatrist in the world like a puppy licking your face.

BERN WILLIAMS

WHEN THE MOON FOLLOWS ME

BY
MARY E. POTTER

Each of my sons made the discovery early. We would be riding in the car at night, and a little voice would call out from the back seat, "Hey, the moon is following us!" I would explain that the moon was not actually gliding along with our car. There would be another period of critical observation and the final verdict, delivered more quietly this time: "But it really *is* moving. I can see it."

I thought of that one evening as I was driving. The moon, one day short of fullness, rode with me, first gliding smoothly, then bouncing over the bumpy stretches, now on my right, then straight ahead, the silver light washing over dry grasses in open fields, streaking along through black branches, finally disappearing as the road wound its way through the hills.

When I crested the hill in the village, there it was again—grown suddenly immense, ripe, flooding the town with a sprawling light so magical I began to understand why it is said to inspire "looniness." I could hardly wait to get back home to show the boys.

Robert was in the bathtub, so I grabbed John. "Close your eyes and come see what followed me home," I said, hoping to increase the dramatic impact. I led him out into the night. "Okay. Open! Isn't it beautiful?"

John blinked a few times and looked at me. "Mom, it's just the moon. Is this the surprise?" I suppose he was hoping for a puppy.

I should have realized that, being only ten, he was probably too young to know how much we sometimes need the magic and romance of moonlight—a light that is nothing like the harsh glare of the sun. Moonlight softens our faults; all shabbiness dissolves into shadow. It erases the myriad details that crowd in the sunlight, leaving only highlights and broad brushstrokes—the fundamental shape of things.

Often in the soothing, restorative glow we stare transfixed, bouncing our ambitions and hopes and plans off this great reflector. We dream our dreams; we examine the structure of our lives; we make considered decisions. In a hectic, confusing world, it helps to step out into a quiet, clear swath of moonlight, to seek out the fundamentals and eschew the incidentals.

The night after I showed John the moon, he burst breathlessly through the door, calling, "Mom, come out for a minute!" This time, he led me, coatless and shivering. The driveway gravel crunched underneath our sneakers. From somewhere in the woods beyond the pond, the plaintive calls of geese honked and died away.

Past the row of pine trees that line the road, the sky opened up with the full moon on it, suspended so precariously close that it might come hurtling toward us—incandescent, even larger and more breathtaking than the night before, climbing its motionless climb over the molten silver of our pond. Even a ten-year-old could see this wasn't just the moon. This was The Moon.

When I turned around, John was grinning, expectant, studying my face intently to see if he had pleased me. He had. I knew that now the moon was following him too.

Even a
ten-year-
ld
was The
Moon.

SISTER SMOG AND THE WINDSHIELD VIPER

BY
JO COUDERT

Her hands whitely clenched in her habit, Sister Michael of God approached the garbage can filled with snakes. "Help yourself, Sister!" the man boomed, his eyes crinkling with amusement. "Pick a good one!"

Sister Michael thought she might faint. Or scream. The wonder was, considering how she felt about snakes, that she was there at all.

Perhaps it was God's doing. After all, how often does a member of a hermit order of nuns listen to the radio? And why, when she turned on the news, did she just happen to hear the announcement for the 1984 Saint Patrick's Day Snake Race?

The event would be held in San Francisco. Snakes (nonpoisonous, of course) would be supplied, and any charitable organization could enter. But Sister Michael wasn't really listening to the announcer. Her mind was on termites.

Termites were feasting on the small wooden houses, scattered over ten acres of hillside, where the nuns lived. That very morning, the exterminator had said that it would cost at least a thousand dollars to repair the damage and get rid of the termites. Where would the nuns find the money?

"First prize is $2000!" the announcer said. Sister Michael snapped to attention. Her eyes went heavenward. *Oh, no, God. You can't really expect me to have anything to do with snakes.* But just in case he did, she sent for an entry blank.

When the form arrived, Sister reluctantly filled it out. Name of entrant? If she put down "Sister Michael of God," that would really commit her. Yet her initials, S.M.O.G., would look silly. So she compromised: "Sister Smog." Name of snake? Goodness, she thought, does it really have to have a name? Well, in that case . . . "Windshield Viper," she wrote, smiling.

Sister Michael mailed the form, a safe enough act since the Hermitage of Christ the King is in Sebastopol, California, and she had no way of getting the 50 miles to San Francisco.

When, on Saint Patrick's Day, friends volunteered to drive her, Sister kept praying for a flat tire. But God had other plans.

The scene in Crown Zellerbach Plaza was festive. Flags were flapping in the breeze; TV cameramen were setting up; the stands were filling with excited spectators.

Sister Michael felt like an early Christian martyr on her way into Rome's Colosseum. "Don't hold the snake too tightly," said a fellow competitor. "I did that last year, and it bit me." Sister had no intention of holding the snake too tightly. Or too loosely. Or any way at all.

Once registered, Sister Michael had been given a wooden dowel ("For tapping the table, not the snake"), a piece of cardboard ("In case the snake goes the wrong way"), a green-plastic derby ("To get you in the spirit of things"), and instructions to pick out her snake.

Perching the green derby on top of her headgear, Sister Michael edged toward the snake-filled garbage can. Withdrawing a shoe box

from under her arm, she asked the man, "Would you mind picking out one with a good personality and putting it in this box?"

He reached calmly into the can and came up with a 20-inch gopher snake. "Hey, what've you got in there?" he asked as he placed the thrashing snake in the box.

"A hot-water bottle. Someone told me snakes like to be warm."

The man hooted. "You'll cook him!"

Sister Michael waited anxiously for the races to begin. First would come preliminary heats, then the semifinals and finals. Suddenly the loudspeaker boomed: "In Lane Four, Sister Smog racing Windshield Viper!" Laughter, followed by a loud cheer, came from the bleachers. Sister waved her derby and advanced to the 18-foot-long racing table. She gingerly snatched the lid from her box and shook Windshield Viper out into Lane Four.

The snake lay motionless. "Oh, dear, what have I done to you?" she murmured miserably, thinking she had roasted him. The announcer's voice came over the loudspeaker: "On your mark. Get set." Hastily, Sister drew a vial of holy water from under her habit and sprinkled the snake's tail.

As the announcer shouted "Slither!" a roar went up from the bleachers. "Windshield Viper in the lead!" the announcer called. "Snake Hips coming up fast in Lane Three!"

Viper raised himself to look over the partition between lanes. Sister blocked his view with the cardboard. He stuck his tongue out at her. Snake Hips passed him. Sister banged frantically on the table with her dowel.

"Windshield Viper takes the lead! Windshield Viper wins by a length!"

Sister ran around the table, grabbed Viper, and slid him into the box.

"Did I really do that?" she said to herself moments later. "Barehanded, I picked up a snake?"

Sitting down heavily, she tried to remember how the snake had felt. Not cold, clammy, or slimy. But dry and clean to the touch. Odd, but Viper didn't seem so frightening now.

Poor thing, she thought. *I must have scared him to death with the holy water. No wonder he stuck out his tongue. He's probably as frightened of me as I am of him.*

Their semifinal heat was called. Sweeping the lid off the shoe box with a flourish, Sister Smog poured Windshield Viper onto the table.

"On your mark! Get set! Slither!" Seconds later, they'd won again. They were in the finals!

Sister held Windshield Viper gently. With one of his beautiful green eyes, the snake seemed to wink at her and tried to curl around her arm. "Now, now," she said. "You did well, but none of that." After admiring the yellow-and-brown pattern on his back, Sister popped him back onto the hot-water bottle in the box. "Warm up for the last race," she told him.

"Now, for the finals. In Lane Two, Sister Smog and Windshield Viper!"

Sliding the snake out onto the starting line, Sister whispered, "Remember the termites, Viper." Leaning closer, she was sure she saw Viper's mouth curved into a smile.

"On your mark! Get set! Slither!"

"Go, Viper, go!" Sister screamed. He hesitated—then curled up. Sister blew on the back of his neck, something she had seen a competitor do.

Suddenly, Viper raised up, surveyed the finish line, and glided forward. "They're neck and neck! Gus and Windshield Viper into the home stretch! It's Gus! It's Windshield Viper! It's Gus! And the winner is . . . Gus!"

Sister ran around the table and picked up Viper. He stuck his tongue out at her. "Yes, I know. You'd have won if I'd been a better handler. But don't feel bad. We'll get the money somewhere."

"Congratulations, Sister. Come over here. Here he is, folks, Windshield Viper! Winner of one thousand dollars!"

"What?"

"Second prize, Sister. You've won a thousand dollars."

"Hey, W.V., did you hear that? Enough for the termites!" A green eye flashed. "Oh, you smart snake. You knew it all the time!"

When the TV interview was finished, some of the kids came over to Sister Smog. "How did you dare hold the snake?" one girl asked.

"Well, I found out that he's like the rest of God's creatures," Sister said. "He likes to be treated warmly."

"Why did you call him Windshield Viper? Weren't you afraid he'd just go side to side?"

"Oh, I never thought of that. You know what I should have called him? Julius Squeezer. He came, he saw, he conquered."

With the $1000 check safely tucked in her habit, Sister returned Viper to the man who had picked him out. "I don't want anything to happen to him," she told him.

"Nothing will. I'll release all the snakes in the nature preserve where I caught them."

As she reached into the shoe box, Sister Michael said, "Thanks, Viper, for teaching me about snakes. I won't be afraid of them again if you won't be afraid of nuns in green derby hats."

As Windshield Viper slid into the garbage can, his green eyes were smiling. Sister Michael of God is quite sure of it.

I've always regarded nature as the clothing of God.

ALAN HOVHANESS

SURE IS COLD

BY
NICK JANS

It's too cold to walk slowly. Smoke from stovepipes curls upward, freezes, and sags back to earth. Drifting in a dense, crystalline pall, the ice fog wraps the village of Ambler, Alaska, in its own frozen breath. As I hurry up the dark street, parka hood drawn, I trail my own white plume.

The winter solstice has passed. Somewhere around noon, dawn sagged into dusk—the edge of a night 20 hours long. Day after day the sky remains pale and featureless. It's too cold to snow, too cold for wind to blow, too cold, it seems, for the sun to rise.

If I could sleep through and wake up in March, I would. I've heard newcomers claim that winter doesn't bother them. If they last three years (and most don't), they keep their claims to themselves.

Eighteen years ago in Machias, Maine, I slammed the door of my grandfather's old '66 Plymouth Belvedere and headed for Alaska. As I rattled 5000 miles across the continent, pistons wheezing, I told myself that Grandpa Paul would have approved. The son of an immigrant, he'd have known why I'd shoved my last 400 bucks in my pocket and fled from a future that looked all too certain.

In Fairbanks I put the car, which I privately called Grandpa's Ghost, up on blocks and canoed off into a new life, finally settling in Ambler, in the northwestern corner of the state.

The questions from my parents started a year later, their voices echoing over the satellite phone. What was I doing up there, hauling water in buckets and using an outhouse? When was I going to get on with my life? When was I coming home?

"I don't know. Next year," I said, believing the sound of my own voice. But a year became five, then ten. The real question wasn't what or when, but why. I knew they didn't quite understand what held me here.

On the upper Kobuk River, first snow flies in mid-September. By month's end it feels like winter: ice floes grinding down the river; gray, stormy days; mornings of sharp cold. The intoxicating, eternal light of summer falls away with startling rapidity, losing five, seven, then 11 minutes a day.

By early November the river is rock-hard, the sun barely clears the Waring Mountains, and we're still losing light. Then the serious cold begins. I wake up shivering one dark morning, and a flashlight on the outside thermometer shows 30 below zero. The water bucket in the corner of my cabin has a skim of ice.

Until April, keeping warm will take constant effort. The wood stove roars at a full draft, roasting my back while my feet freeze. My Eskimo neighbors sum it up in a single exclamation—*Alappaa!* It's cold!

In deep cold the laws of physics seem warped. Wood on the chopping block shatters beneath the axe; steel snaps like plastic. If you want to start your snowmobile, you pour boiling water on the manifold to coax gasoline into vaporizing.

Getting dressed and undressed takes extra time. Like everyone else, I live in layers of acrylic fleece, goose down, and fur. Full winter gear—20 pounds of long johns, insulated pants, coveralls, parka, face mask, beaver cap and mitts, Army surplus "bunny boots"—feels like walking around in football equipment padded with blankets.

The worst usually comes in January. Temperatures fall to 60, even 70 below and stay there for weeks. Although my log cabin is snug, frost coats the door hinges, builds half an inch thick on windows, creeps up from the floor on inside walls. Life curls inward like a sled dog in the snow, cradling its embers.

But no matter how cold it gets, the Ambler school where I teach doesn't close. There are church services and town meetings. Eskimos hunt, cut wood, and travel between villages in all but the worst cold snaps, as they've always done. Whether it's their diet (rich in animal fat and protein) or sheer toughness, the Eskimos shrug off weather that could kill an outsider. Bareheaded teenagers walk to school in letter jackets and basketball shoes; hunters bear purple-black frostbite scars as badges of honor.

But it's easy enough to pull on another sweater, stuff another log in the stove. What gets me is the darkness. It gnaws from the inside, day after day, month after month. On a bad day even caribou chili tastes like cardboard. People in the Lower 48 might call it cabin fever. Scientists who study such things chatter about SAD—seasonal affective disorder. Around here people simply call it what it is: The Darkness.

In the dim light and paralyzing cold, I wonder what possesses me to live in the Arctic anyway. I forget the day, just three months before, when I sat transfixed on the Hunt River tundra, watching thousands of caribou flow by, or the simple joy of watching my seventh-graders excited by an art project.

I sleep ten hours a day and down quarts of coffee to stay functional. My only consolation is experience. I remind myself over and over that I'm not going crazy, and everyone else is fighting The Darkness too.

A homesteader who lived out in the country for 20 years once told me, "It's a cumulative effect. The winters pile up on top of each other, and finally the question is how many you can take." It's no coincidence that he and his wife moved to Hawaii. Others have opted for Arizona or California. No one who spends 20 years in the Arctic moves to Minnesota or Montana. Ever.

In March a blizzard sweeps in. Snow stings like sand, piles in waist-high drifts. There's nothing to do but stay indoors and wait it out. After two days the wind fades into an afternoon of dreamlike calm and clarity. The mountains glow, and the promise of spring is in the air. I turn to catch the sun on my face, to feel the light within. Although two months of snow and cold lie ahead, it's over. The Darkness has passed.

Outside the school, kids in T-shirts throw snowballs. Regina Randall, the school secretary, smiles as she walks by. "Nice and warm, eh?"

"Sure is," I reply.

It's ten below zero.

And if Grandpa could see where his Ghost had carried me, maybe he'd smile and nod.

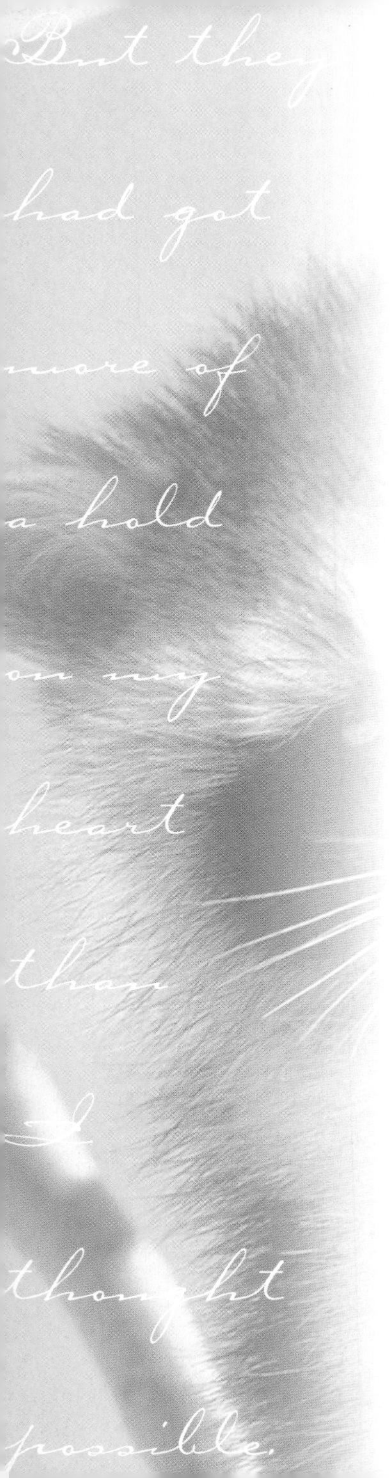

SUMMER OF THE RACCOONS

BY
FRED BAUER

If I'd had my way, the story would have ended that spring day where it began—on the sixth hole at Stony Brook. "What was that bawling?" my wife Shirley asked, interrupting me in mid-backswing. Without another word she marched into a mucky undergrowth and re-emerged carrying something alive.

"Rrrit, rrit, rrit," it screamed.

"It's an orphaned raccoon," she said, gently stroking a mud-matted ball of gray fur.

"Its mother is probably ten yards away, has rabies, and is about to attack," I scolded.

"No, it's alone and starving—that's why the little thing is out of its nest. Here, take it," she ordered. "I think there's another baby over there."

In a minute she returned with a squalling bookend—just as mud-encrusted and emaciated as the first. She wrapped the two complaining ingrates in her sweater. I knew that look. We were going to have two more mouths to feed.

"Just remember," I declared, "they're your bundles to look after." But of all the family proclamations I have made over the years, none was wider of the mark.

When, like Shirley and me, you have four children, you don't think much about empty nests. You don't think the exuberant procession of kids and their friends will ever end. But the bedrooms will someday empty, the hot water will miraculously return, and the sounds that make a family will echo only in the scrapbook of your mind.

Shirley and I had gone through the parting ritual with Laraine and Steve and Christopher. Now there was only Daniel, who was chafing to trade his room at home for a pad at Penn State. So I was looking forward to my share of a little peace and quiet—not raccoons.

"What do you feed baby raccoons?" I asked the game protector over the phone the next morning. We had cleaned them up, made them a bed in a box of rags, found old baby bottles in the basement, fed them warm milk, and got them to sleep, all without floorwalking the first night.

However, they revived and began their machine-gun chant shortly after Shirley had run out the door, heading for classes. In anticipation of a soon-to-be empty nest, she had gone back to college to get a master's degree so she could teach.

Meanwhile, I had my own work to do—various publishing projects that I handle from home. As the only child remaining with us, Daniel was my potential raccoon-relief man. Or so I hoped.

"Whose bright idea was this?" he asked with the tart tongue of a teenager.

"Your mother thought you needed something more to earn your allowance," I cracked. "Will you heat some milk for them?"

"Sorry, I'm late for school," he called over his shoulder. He and I were at that awkward testing stage, somewhere between my flagging authority and his rush for independence.

The major problem in trying to feed the raccoons was one of flow. Milk was flowing out of the bottle too fast and through the kits the same way.

"Thinner milk and less corn syrup," the wildlife man suggested. "The object," he coached, "is to take care of them until they can go back to the woods and take care of themselves."

"I'll do anything I can to make that happen," I assured him. "They're about eight ounces each"—I had weighed them on my postage scale. "They'll be old enough to be on their own in a couple of weeks, right?"

"Not quite," he said. "Come fall, if all goes well, they'll be ready."

I'll strangle them before then, I said under my breath. I prepared a new formula and tried it on one. The kit coughed and sputtered like a clogged carburetor. The hole in the nipple was too big.

Maybe I could feed them better with a doll's bottle, I concluded, and set out to find one. At a toy store, I found some miniature bottles, one of which was attached to a specially plumbed doll named Betsy Wetsy. "My Betsys are wetsy enough," I told the clerk—declining doll and diapers, but taking the bottle.

Back home, I tried feeding the raccoons again. Miracle of miracles, they sucked contentedly and fell asleep. (Only 12 more weeks to September, I counted down.)

During the next month and a half, I functioned faithfully as day-care nanny for Bonnie and Clyde, named for their bandit-like masks. The kits apparently considered me their mother. When I held them at feeding time, they still spoke in the same scratchy voice, but now it was a contented hum. They only time they may have perceived me to be an imposter came when they climbed on my shoulders, parted my hair, and pawed in vain for a nipple.

Before long the kits graduated to cereal and bananas. When they became more active, our backyard birdbath became an instant attraction. Bonnie, the extrovert of the two, ladled the water worshipfully with her paws like a priest conducting a baptism. Clyde followed suit, but cautiously, as if the water might be combustible. Next Bonnie discovered the joy of food and water together, and thereafter every morsel had to be dipped before being eaten.

By July the kits weighed about three pounds. I built a screened-in cage and moved them outdoors. When they had adjusted well to their new quarters, Daniel suggested we free them to explore the woods and forage for food.

"I don't want them to get lost or hurt out there," I said, sounding more like a mother hen than a surrogate father raccoon.

"They should get used to being on their own," Daniel insisted. We left their door ajar so they could wander during the day. At night, we called them home by banging together their food bowls. They came out of the woods at a gallop.

Still I was afraid we might be rushing their initiation to the wild. One windy afternoon while Daniel and I were playing catch in the backyard, I spotted Bonnie, 20 feet off the ground, precariously tightrope-walking the bouncing branches of a mulberry tree. She had eaten her fill of berries and was trying to get down, I thought.

"Be careful, Babe," I called, running to the tree. "Quick, Dan, get a ladder!"

"Let her go," he said calmly. "She's on an adventure. Don't spoil her fun." And he was on the money. When I returned later, she was snoozing serenely in the mulberry's cradling arms.

However, the raccoons did get into trouble one night when they let themselves out of their cage with those dexterous forepaws. Shirley and I were awakened at 2:00 A.M. by a horrendous scream.

"What was that?" I asked, bolting upright.

"The raccoons?" she wondered.

"They're in trouble!" Tossing off the covers, I grabbed a flashlight and ran outside in my skivvies.

As I came around the south side of the house, I heard something rattle the eaves and jump into the maple tree. Next, I got jumped. First, by Bonnie landing on my shoulder, followed by her brother shinnying up my leg. Circling my neck, they jabbered their excitement: *"Rrrrit, rrrrit, rrrrit!"*

Animals are nothing but the visible reflections of our souls. God displays them to us to give us food for thought.

VICTOR HUGO

"It's okay, I've got ya, you're safe," I said, cuddling them in my arms. Apparently a wild raccoon, defending its territory, had attacked Clyde. He had a bloody shoulder that didn't appear serious; Bonnie was fine.

July gave way to August, and August to September. Soon the days were getting shorter, and the raccoons were six-pound butterballs. I was fascinated by their creativity and intelligence. One evening after I banged their food bowls together, there was no reply. When I reported anxiously at the breakfast table that they hadn't come in the night before, Daniel laughed at my concern.

"Now we'll see if you're as good a teacher as a mother raccoon."

"I already know the answer," I said. "By the way, what time did you get in last night?"

"About midnight," he answered.

"Your eyes say later."

"I'm not a baby anymore," he shot back.

Outside, I beckoned the raccoons again, and this time they reported: effervescent Bonnie in a flat-out sprint, Clyde in a tag-along amble.

Near the end of September they were missing a week, and I suggested to Shirley that they were probably gone for good.

"You know it's a mistake trying to hold on to anything that no longer needs you," she counseled.

"Who's holding on?" I protested. But when I continued scanning the woods, hoping to catch sight of them, I knew she was right. Reluctantly, I dismantled their pen and put them out of my mind. Or tried to. But they had got more of a hold on my heart than I thought possible. What I had considered a nuisance had, in fact, been a gift; what I had labeled a burden, a blessing. Why is it, I asked myself, that with so many people and things, we only appreciate them fully after they're gone?

One Saturday near the end of October, Shirley, Daniel, and I were in the backyard raking leaves when I spotted a ringed tail beyond the gate that opens to the woods. "Look, Shirley," I whispered. And though I had no idea if it was one of ours, I called, "Bonnie, Clyde."

The magnificently marked animal rose on its hind legs and looked us over inquisitively. For a frozen moment, we faced off, statue-like. Then I called again, and the animal moved in our direction. It was Bonnie, and we went to meet her. Kneeling, I held out my hand, which she licked while I rubbed her neck. She purred her most satisfied *rrrrit, rrrrit, rrrrit.*

"Go get a banana for her," I suggested to Daniel.

"No, it's time she made it on her own," he replied firmly. "She's a big girl now. Don't do anything for her that she can do for herself."

I looked at Shirley and winked. Tall, broad-shouldered Daniel wasn't talking raccoons. He was talking parents. *The object is to take care of them until they can take care of themselves,* a haunting voice echoed. It was time to let go.

After rubbing Bonnie's neck one last time, I stepped back. She sensed my release and bounded off joyfully in the direction from which she had come.

"Have a good life," I called after her. Then she dipped behind a tree and was gone.

"DID I COME THIS FAR TO DIE?"

BY
SHELDON KELLY

On the night of February 4, 1982, Doris Callahan was awakened in her Dover, Massachusetts, home by a terrible vision of her son Steven. At the time of the revelation, Steven was sailing alone in a small yacht in the mid-Atlantic. "I could actually see him," Doris told her husband, Edgar. "He was clawing up through dark, murky water."

Doris tried to set her dream aside. For Steven, the nightmare was just beginning.

It was nearing midnight when Steven Callahan, twenty-nine, lay down on the bunk of his 22-foot sloop *Napoleon Solo*. In the seven days since leaving the Canary Islands, off the coast of Africa, he had sailed 800 miles. This was the last leg of his round-trip crossing of the Atlantic, a demanding test for the boat he had designed and built as the prototype of a small ocean-cruising yacht. With fair winds he would reach the Caribbean island of Antigua ahead of his scheduled arrival date of February 24. But tonight, February 4, a storm was brewing.

Suddenly, there was a tremendous crash against the hull. In seconds Callahan was waist-deep in water, and the boat seemed about to sink. He grabbed a knife and tried to cut loose his survival duffel. The boat listed more steeply. *She's going down,* he thought, *taking me with her!* He broke through the hatch. Waves lapped over the deck, and the bow was completely submerged.

Callahan cut loose the life raft, then jerked the cord to inflate it. Placing the knife between his teeth, he leaped to the raft as the mast's anticollision strobe light short-circuited and began flashing surreal shadows against the roiling ocean.

Floating close to the sinking boat, Callahan cut away a section of the mainsail, and grabbed two floating cabbages and a coffee can. *It would not be enough!* His life depended upon getting that survival duffel. He tied the raft to the stern, reboarded, and then ducked into the pitch-black water that filled the cabin.

He surfaced for air several times as he cut away at the duffel tie-downs. Finally he freed the bag. When he turned to leave, the hatch was sealed shut by water. *This is it!* Callahan thought. He clawed at the escape route, struggling for his life.

Suddenly, the hatch blew open, and Callahan emerged, gasping for air. He boarded the raft and tied a long cord to the stern of *Solo*. If the ship remained afloat, he would reboard her in the morning and gather more provisions.

Just before dawn, the cord snapped. Callahan watched as the mast's flashing light grew smaller, then vanished. Adrift on a tiny raft, he thought first of trying to keep warm, and then of the creature—probably a whale—that had shattered the sloop's hull.

The sky remained dark and rainy throughout the day. Waves rose to 20 feet in gale-force winds, often completely submerging the seven-foot, circular raft. Callahan bailed with his salvaged coffee can. Saltwater sores had developed on his knees and elbows; deep cuts on his thighs and back—suffered in *Solo*'s flooded cabin—made movement painful. During lulls, he took stock of what were now his life's most precious possessions.

He began to pray awkwardl spelling out his thoughts and hopes.

Included in the survival duffel were three pounds of food, ten days' supply of water, a spear gun, a beacon-sending radio, ropes and cords, a Boy Scout utensil set, two flashlights, and three solar water stills—each capable of producing by condensation about a pint of fresh water daily. He also had a rocket gun, flares and an air pump, a plastic box containing navigational charts, and a sea-survival book.

Callahan listened to the signals being broadcast from his radio and studied the chart. He was 350 miles east of the nearest shipping lanes, drifting in a north equatorial current, and weeks away from potential rescue. The survival manual stated that one could live 30 days without food, but only ten without water. The solar stills would not function, so Callahan limited himself to a half pint of water daily. He ate sparingly.

His thoughts drifted home to his parents, his two brothers and sister, and his small farm and boat-building shop in Lamoine, Maine. *I'm going to survive,* he vowed. *Somehow, I'm going to make it.*

After 36 hours of steady SOS signals, Callahan shut off the radio, knowing that no one could hear the beeps.

The storm finally ended four days later. During lulls in the weather, Callahan had spotted an occasional dorado. Now the number of fish around the raft grew, circling, leaping, always just out of spear-gun range. Although the solar stills hadn't yet functioned and his food supplies were almost gone, Callahan was heartened by the presence of the dorados. They represented life, food, and even companionship.

While the dorados cavorted, Callahan worked feverishly on the stills, stopping occasionally to study the chart and to log notations. Calculating his approximate speed by timing the passage of heavy seaweed, he believed he was averaging 15 to 30 miles every 24 hours. His direction was checked nightly by sighting the North Star and the Southern Cross, and rechecked daily by marking the positions of the rising and setting sun. By lashing pencils into a crude sextant sighted simultaneously on the North Star and the horizon, he had calculated his latitude. He was attempting to reach the shipping lanes and the Caribbean.

Suddenly a large shark approached and began tearing at the ballast tanks—water-filled pockets hanging below the raft. Callahan jabbed it fiercely with the spear gun until it retreated. He had never felt more alone. Yet, whenever he looked, the dorados were there, swimming ever closer to the raft.

Doris Callahan could not shake the vision. "I won't rest," she told the family, "until the twenty-fourth arrives and I know that Steven is safe."

On his tenth day adrift, Callahan spear-gunned a spiny triggerfish. The next day he speared his first dorado. That night he feasted on the delicious meat, and during the following days he extracted every ounce of fluid and meat from the fish, eating eyes, organs, roe. Maybe he could survive—if the dorados stayed with him.

On the fourteenth day, the solar stills began producing water. Sharks often hit the raft during the night, but he drove them away by the sharp prods of the spear gun. After each attack, his fears for the raft increased.

Every third or fourth day Callahan managed to spear-gun another of his treasured dorados. When the rubber band that released the spear from the gun broke, he lashed the shaft of the spear to the gun, making it into a handheld spear. The dorados moved closer—as if to allow him to make the kill. He was profoundly moved. *They are actually helping me,* he thought.

On the eighth of March, 12 days after his scheduled arrival, Callahan's family reported to the U.S. Coast Guard that he was missing. A check of possible ports of departure and arrival was begun, and ships were notified. When no trace of the boat was found by March 17, the Coast Guard called off the search.

The following week, the Callahans' oldest son, thirty-four-year-old Edgar, Jr.—once a commercial deep-sea fisherman—arrived from Hawaii. He immediately organized a search center in the family kitchen. "If I know Steve," he said, "he hasn't given up. We've just got to locate his position."

In his log, Callahan carefully noted navigation, water and food intake, and weather conditions. Should he die and the raft wash ashore, the data might prove valuable. *Perhaps that is my reason for existence,* he thought wildly. *To drift at sea, suffering until no more suffering can be borne, so that others may learn of man's limitations.*

> *Nature is often hidden, sometimes overcome, seldom extinguished.*
>
> FRANCIS BACON

I cannot live another week, he thought one baking-hot afternoon. Then, standing painfully to search the horizon for ships, he saw a full rainbow, inset with a smaller one. Its beauty on the glistening sea overwhelmed him. Callahan had never been particularly religious, but at that moment he believed he saw the scheme of nature, the beauty and the horror, all fitting strangely into life's cycle. He began to pray, awkwardly, spelling out his thoughts and hopes.

On March 20, disaster struck. While he was hauling in a dorado, the spear gun's shaft broke, ripping a hole in the raft's side. Then a storm hit. Callahan tried closing the hole with line after plugging it with foam from the boat cushion. It continued to leak and he had to pump air and bail throughout the day and night. Exhausted, he began pacing himself, allowing brief moments of sleep before resuming his life-and-death struggle.

On the third night following the accident, as Callahan worked with a flashlight tied to his forehead, a large shark zipped by. At dawn the shark was still there, circling. "He knows that I'm getting weak," Callahan said to himself.

Four days later, his fifty-second adrift, the storm grew in intensity. He noted in his log: "My body is rotting away before my eyes." He broke down, screaming in frustration, then crying, "O Lord, did I come this far to die?" He lay beneath the canopy sobbing as the bottom tube of the raft deflated. Several moments later he struggled to his raw knees and began anew to pump air into the damaged tube. Again the foam plug was blown out. He knew this was his last chance; he'd better find a solution or he would die.

Then the answer came to him: Remove the handle from the Boy Scout utensil fork and put it through the top edge, the foam plug, and the bottom edge. Tie off the tear and the handle will hold the lashing in place. It worked; the foam plug held.

Several hours later, the storm ended and the dorados clustered near the bow. Callahan held the spear gun ready, too weak to strike a killing blow, yet desperately in need of food. His body was deteriorating. His sores were not healing; his fingernails had loosened. A dorado approached, then rolled over on its back, revealing its soft underbelly. Callahan killed it easily, thankfully.

Edgar Callahan, Jr., worked night and day studying the drift pattern and weather data in order to project probable conditions and the path of Steve's raft. He finally figured that Steve had to be within a 200-mile quadrant northeast of the group of islands that rims the Caribbean Sea. Several days later it was reported that Solo*'s wreckage had been found on a Puerto Rican shore. The Callahan family cried and prayed together, but decided not to give up. "I'm certain," insisted Edgar, Sr. "Steve is alive." He even thought about selling the house to finance a private search operation.*

On April 21, day 76, three black frigate birds appeared above the raft. The water turned a deeper blue; the dorados were joined by other fish. Soon Callahan saw the outline of steep cliffs. As he drifted nearer, he spotted a barrier of coral reef pounded by violent surf. It could cut him to shreds. He stripped plastic and foam from the boat cushion, hoping that it, along with the piece of mainsail, might offer some protection against the coral. Now, a few hundred yards ahead, lay the final test of his 2600-mile ordeal.

Suddenly, a fishing boat raced into view. Callahan waved frantically, and the boat headed for the raft. Three fishermen from Marie Galante, a tiny islet 80 miles south of Antigua, were astounded by what they saw: leaping dorados surrounded the raft. It seemed as if the long-haired, bearded man inside the circle was their master!

What had brought the fishermen to that area at that moment? They had seen the birds, which signaled fish, hovering out to sea. And what brought the birds? The dorados again, always the dorados.

Although suffering from serious malnutrition, dehydration, exposure, multiple sores, and wounds, Callahan was lucid, giving his name in a parched whisper. He weighed 40 pounds less than normal. Yet several hours after being carried ashore he could stand without assistance.

Fishermen and villagers sought him out during his recuperation. They gathered outside his hotel room, waiting for the chance to see him, "the great fisherman that God brought back."

The plentiful dorado meat had kept him alive for his 76-day ordeal. But to Steve Callahan they were more than food. "The whole experience with them was mystical, even spiritual," he says today. "What they did for me borders on the miraculous."

There is a pleasure in the pathless wood,

There is a rapture on the lonely shore

There is society, where none intrudes,

By the deep Sea, and Music in its roar:

I love not Man the less, but Nature more.

LORD BYRON

THE DAY OF THE BEAR

BY
PER OLA AND EMILY D'AULAIRE

In late 1986 Missy Perkins spotted an ad for a free, three-year-old spayed female mongrel that had outgrown its owners' home. The dog seemed an ideal solution to an ongoing problem.

The ducks and chickens on the Perkinses' small Vermont farm were being gobbled up by weasels, foxes, and raccoons. The vegetables succumbed to rabbits and deer. The right dog might keep the varmints away. Besides, Missy, her husband, Dale, and their five children were confirmed animal lovers, and a pooch would be a welcome addition to the family.

Missy phoned the owner, who said she would bring the dog to the farm the next day. When Missy saw the animal, she wondered if she'd made a mistake. It was an 80-pound, shaggy beast—half Newfoundland and half "something that came out of the woodpile." Missy worried that the dog's dense coat would spread the smell of the barnyard to all corners of their farmhouse.

But the dog let the kids tug on its fur and pull its ears without a growl. It seemed placid yet alert, affectionate and well-adjusted. And though an animal that big would have an appetite to match, the Perkinses had enough yield from their own livestock to provide plenty of scraps for the dog to eat.

But something nagged at Missy. The dog's owners must have realized the pup was destined to be big, since they knew it was half Newfoundland, a breed that can tip the scales at over 150 pounds. They *must* have foreseen that it would outgrow their home. Was there another reason the owners were giving it away? Was there something about this dog that they wouldn't tell?

For the children it was love at first sight, and they pleaded to keep the animal. Missy relented, provided the pooch would be returned if things didn't work out.

The dog's name was Rosie, but not for long. "She isn't a rose," declared three-year-old Zeke of the woolly creature with floppy ears and paws like bedroom slippers. "She looks more like a bear." By dinner that evening, Rosie had become The Bear.

For a while Missy still asked herself what the real reason was that the dog had been given away. But The Bear didn't chew things or chase cars, and she seemed to understand that her job was to protect the other animals. She guarded the children as well, watching over them as closely as she did the chickens and ducks. In winter the dog galloped alongside the children as they sledded down snowy hills. In summer she swam with them in a nearby river.

Newfoundlands have a keen instinct for water rescue, a trait bred into them over the centuries by Atlantic fishermen, who used them to help haul in nets and save men overboard. The Bear's heritage was evident: when the children plunged into the river, the dog swam in circles around them, barking when she felt they ventured out too far. She was the perfect farm dog—companion, guardian, protector.

From the outset, the dog's favorite among the children was Zeke. As soon as the school bus disappeared down the road with the four

For the children it was love at first sight, and they pleaded to keep the anima older children, Zeke and The Bear headed for the barn with Missy to milk the cows.

After lunch the two often curled up in the kitchen near the wood-burning stove. Sometimes The Bear would doze while Zeke pretended to read to her. Often both were sound asleep, a tangle of dark fur, blond hair, small hands, and huge paws. At bedtime, Zeke saved his last hug for The Bear, his "best friend."

On December 19, 1987, Missy had left the farm to drop off ten-year-old Becky for Christmas caroling and eleven-year-old Josh at a friend's house. The three younger children were playing outside in the snow with The Bear. As their father walked to the house from the mail-box, eight-year-old Martha asked is she, Zeke, and Sarah could slide on the pond.

There are two small spring-fed ponds on the Perkins property. For several days now the weather had been bone-warping cold, and both ponds had frozen almost to the bottom.

Dale gave the kids his okay, then went into the house. Martha, Sarah, and Zeke slid back and forth, but after a few minutes Sarah announced that she was growing bored. "Let's go over and slide on Lee's Pond," she suggested.

Lee's Pond, some 250 yards away, hidden from the Perkins house by a row of trees, had been scooped out of a hayfield by a farmer to provide water for his cattle. About 70 feet across, the pond had banks that dropped from the shore to a depth of about eight feet. If *their* pond was frozen solid, the kids reasoned, surely the other was too.

Shouting happily, the trio slid back and forth, their boots gliding easily across the ice. They laughed as they watched The Bear's futile attempts to stop suddenly, efforts that would instead send her skidding beyond them. Then, tired, the three sat down on the ice, and The Bear plopped down beside them. Suddenly the ice gave way under their combined weight. As The Bear jumped for shore, the three children plunged into the frigid water.

Shrieking, Martha and Sarah struggled to find footing on submerged stumps and rocks. Branches from a nearby thicket provided handholds, and using every ounce of their strength, the two girls hauled themselves to shore. But little Zeke flailed helplessly in the water, clinging to a broken chunk of ice, unable to crawl onto it.

He yelled for help as Martha and Sarah struggled to reach him, but he was beyond their grasp. Though both the girls could swim, they knew they weren't strong enough to stay afloat with their wet, heavy clothing.

Zeke's swimming abilities were minimal. The more he thrashed, the farther out he drifted, his jacket, boots, long underwear, and heavy pants filling with water, threatening to weight him down. Frantically searching for long sticks to slide toward their brother, the girls could find nothing that wasn't solidly rooted to the ground. By now all were yelling in terror.

Missy was away only half an hour. When she returned, she checked in on Dale, then wandered outside to make sure the kids were warm enough. They weren't on the little ponds as she had expected, so she headed for the barn. Halfway there she heard screams coming from the direction of Lee's Pond.

Praying she'd get there in time, Missy sprinted across the field, calling out her children's names. "Answer me, Martha!" she screamed. "Zeke? Are you there? Sarah, answer me!" With the nearest neighbor about a quarter-mile away, she knew it was unlikely that anyone would have seen or heard the children.

Zeke's grip on the ice weakened. "Hang on!" cried his sisters. The Bear, who had clambered up on shore, immediately seemed to understand the danger of the situation. She let out a series of woofs and sprang into action, heading straight for Zeke and plunging into the water. She snagged his coat collar, locking it tightly in her teeth. Her grip secure, the dog pulled the terrified youngster toward the bank and into shallow water, where he could stand.

The great pleasure of a dog is that you may make a fool of yourself with him and not only will he not scold you, but he will make a fool of himself too.

SAMUEL BUTLER

Then The Bear did something she'd never done before, and has not done since. She turned around and presented her tail to Zeke. Her message was clear, even to a confused and scared four-year-old. Zeke grabbed the tail, and The Bear towed him toward safety. With a final tug and help from Martha and Sarah, the dog pulled Zeke onto the bank where he sank, sobbing, into his sisters' arms. "Oh Bear, you're the greatest!" Sarah shouted.

When Missy reached the huddled trio, she dropped to her knees and scooped her children into her arms, laughing and crying at the same time. The Bear licked one wet face after another.

At dinner that night the Perkinses joined hands in prayer. They thanked God for each day that they were together. What happened that afternoon gave them all a new awareness of the fragility of life and of the fine line that separates good fortune from misfortune.

Word of The Bear's heroic deed spread, even beyond the Vermont community, and several days later the Perkins kitchen was filled with reporters and television crews. A California animal-welfare group awarded The Bear a gold cup and a red, white, and blue ribbon.

The Bear takes it all in stride, content to guard her chickens, her sheep—and her children. "She just likes being her plain Bear self," says Zeke, putting his arms around the big dog's neck.

Having read about The Bear, the previous owner visited the Perkins farm. Missy mentioned her skepticism over their explanation for giving the big dog away. The animal really was big for her home, the woman said. But then she added sheepishly, "Can you imagine, my father thought she was stupid!"

WHAT I LEARNED ON THE ROAD

BY
CHARLES KURALT

I come from wandering tribes, Norse and Celtic on my mother's side, nomad Bavarians on my father's. All the itinerant impulses of our lineage seem to have concentrated in me.

My family moved from one town to another in eastern North Carolina, and I loved every move. My father's job as field supervisor for the state required him to travel to the small-town county seats, and since my mother was busy teaching school, somebody had to take care of me. The solution—a little troublesome for my father, but perfect for me—was for him to take me along.

We stopped to fish in creeks turned black by tannin from the trees. We stopped for suppers of pork chops, sweet potatoes, and collard greens at roadside cafés. I wanted never to go home.

It was on dirt roads that I learned to drive. Later I nagged my parents to lie about my age so I could get a license three months early. With that precious, fraudulent document in hand, the first thing I did was plan a trip. A friend and I jumped into an ancient rebuilt car and headed for Illinois, where I would go to summer school and my friend would keep the car and get a job.

At the end of summer I hitchhiked home. One of the rides I got was through Kentucky hill country with a kindly evangelist in a pickup that had a loudspeaker atop the cab. He slowed as we passed through each hamlet so he could exhort the citizens to come to God lest sulfur and flame overtake them right there on the street.

I rode contentedly in the back of that pickup with my feet propped up on my suitcase. Watching the mountain curves recede behind me, I returned the wave of a man who stood up from work in his vegetable patch to watch us pass. I saw a barefoot young woman in a calico dress pinning sheets to a clothesline. I saw a cluster of old men studying the moves in a game of checkers on the front porch of a one-pump station. I felt free.

Ever since then I've liked little roads without numbers the best, the bumpy ones that lead over the hills toward vicinities unknown.

In time I went to college, took up journalism, and eventually became a reporter for CBS News. For ten years I covered assignments that taxed my physique and temperament—stories on wars, polar expeditions, politics, and calamities.

Then, in the early fall of 1967, I was flying to Cleveland on one of those cool, clear nights when you can see the lights of all the small towns from miles above.

"Look down there," said my cameraman. "Here we are flying to a story and flying right over ten thousand stories."

"A hundred thousand," I exclaimed, recalling the joys of my driving trips years before.

So when I got back to New York, I went to see Dick Salant, the president of CBS News, with a suggestion: "Why don't you let me just wander for three months to see what I can find?"

"What do you *think* you'll find?" he asked.

I waxed poetic. "Farmers bringing in their crops, first-graders starting school, county fairs, town meetings."

Salant was distracted. "Okay," he said. "But keep the budget down."

So my crew and I set out to wander, without an idea in our heads. I soon discovered it was best to take a deep breath, mosey along, and soak up the moods of the country and the changes of weather and terrain. I didn't have to worry about finding stories. They found me.

In Westerville, Ohio, for example, I met Professor John Franklin Smith, who had taught speech and dramatics at Otterbein College until he reached mandatory retirement age. "I loved my students," he said, "and I think they loved me."

He couldn't imagine leaving the students behind. So when he was forced to retire, he just kept working—for 15 years—as a janitor in the gym.

"I'm still looking ahead," he said. "I don't want to die. There's too much fun in this world. And good books to read and fish to catch and pretty women to admire and good men to know. Why, life is a joy!"

I, too, have found joy abounding in my native land. I rode the Wabash Cannonball through Indiana, and the *Delta Queen* down the Ohio River, and the cable cars up and down the San Francisco hills. I heard jazz in the streets of New Orleans and brass bands in the streets of Bristol, Rhode Island. I saw corncob pipes being made in Washington, Missouri, and windmills being built in Broken Arrow, Oklahoma.

I learned that gas-station attendants are more polite the farther the station is from a main highway. That's how I met M. C. Pinkstaff, roadside poet of a small town in Illinois and proprietor of Pinkstaff's Two-Pump Gas Station and Poem Factory. He sold gasoline—and poems on local topics for ten cents apiece. His best-selling poem was "Morose Maud, the Mule That Kicked Down the Barn Door."

In North Dakota, I found a farmer who explained his marriage of 40 years with "Kissing don't last, but good cooking does." I also learned that "If a honeybee buzzes around your head, you are about to find some money," and "Never kill hogs or dig potatoes in the dark of the moon."

I learned how to say "I don't believe it" politely. In Iowa it's "Could be." In Maine, "I imagine." In Wyoming, "You reckon?" And in Arkansas, "That's a new one on me."

Some stories that I didn't believe at first turned out to be true. Somebody wrote me about a man who lived deep in the woods near the Gunnison River in Colorado, tending a remote power station. The wild birds knew him so well that they'd perch on his shoulder, and the skittish white-tailed deer would come out of the forest to take food from his hand.

It was all true. George Norris had been feeding the deer for many winters. "C'mon, Cutter," he'd say. "You better come runnin', Soap, or all the food will be gone!" And the wild deer would leap the picket fence into his yard, as docile as house pets in the presence of the one man they trusted. A great antlered buck stood nose to nose with Norris and took an oatcake from his mouth.

I am acquainted with people who live settled lives and find deep gratification in family and home. I know now what I've missed, the birthdays and anniversaries, the generations together at the table, the pleasures of kinship, the rituals of the hearth.

Still I wander, seeking compensation in unforeseen encounters and unexpected sights, in sunsets, storms, and passing fancies. I keep thinking I'll find something wonderful just around the next bend. And I always do.

"HAVE YOU SEEN THE TREE?"

BY
ROBERT S. KYFF

My neighbor Mrs. Gargan first told me about it. "Have you seen the tree?" she asked as I was sitting in the backyard enjoying the October twilight.

"The one down at the corner," she explained. "It's a beautiful tree—all kinds of colors. Cars are stopping to look. You ought to see it."

I told her I would, but I soon forgot about the tree. Three days later, I was jogging down the street, my mind swimming with petty worries, when a splash of bright orange caught my eye. For an instant, I thought someone's house had caught fire. Then I remembered the tree.

As I approached it, I slowed to a walk. There was nothing remarkable about the shape of the tree, a medium-sized maple. But Mrs. Gargan had been right about its colors. Like the messy whirl of an artist's palette, the tree blazed a bright crimson on its lower branches, burned with vivid yellows and oranges in its center, and simmered to deep burgundy at its top. Through these fiery colors cascaded thin rivulets of pale-green leaves and blotches of deep-green leaves, as yet untouched by autumn.

Edging closer—like a pilgrim approaching a shrine—I noticed several bare branches near the top, their black twigs scratching the air like claws. The leaves they had shed lay like a scarlet carpet around the trunk.

With its varied nations of color, this tree seemed to become a globe, embracing in its broad branches all seasons and continents: the spring and summer of the Southern Hemisphere in the light and dark greens, the autumn and winter of the Northern in the blazing yellows and bare branches. The whole planet seemed poised on the pivot of this pastiche.

As I marveled at this all-encompassing beauty, I thought of Ralph Waldo Emerson's comments about the stars. If the constellations appeared only once in a thousand years, he observed in *Nature,* imagine what an exciting event it would be. But because they're up there every night, we barely give them a look.

I felt the same way about the tree. Because its majesty will last only a week, it should be especially precious to us. And I had almost missed it.

Once when Emily Dickinson's father noticed a brilliant display of northern lights in the sky over Massachusetts, he tolled a church bell to alert townspeople. That's what I felt like doing about the tree. I wanted to become a Paul Revere of autumn, awakening the countryside to its wonder.

I didn't have a church bell or a horse, but as I walked home, I did ask each neighbor I passed the same simple but momentous question Mrs. Gargan had asked me: "Have you seen the tree?"

October, here's to you. Here's to the heady aroma of the frost-kissed apples, the winey smell of ripened grapes, the wild-as-the-wind smell of hickory nuts and the nostalgic whiff of that first wood smoke.

KEN WEBER

THE MOST WORTHLESS CLASS I EVER TOOK

BY
FRED BAUER

Wisdom comes easy when you're young. At twenty-two, I knew what I wanted and what I liked. And after a couple of years in the Army, I knew I'd had enough of the outdoors to last a lifetime. Others could rhapsodize about the glories of nature, I resolved as I duffel-bagged back to college for my last two years at Bowling Green State University in Ohio. I would get no closer to the wilds than a golf-course rough.

Then suddenly, heading into my last semester, I discovered that I was one science course short of graduation.

"How about a course in ornithology?" my academic adviser suggested.

"Insects?" I queried.

"Birds," he answered. "I understand the class is a lark."

It turned out to be more like a full-scale jungle maneuver. "Here's your reading list, schedule of tests, and field trips," the rotund professor, Everett Myers, announced. I studied the paper, stunned. There were weekly tests, more than a dozen books to read, and field trips to every lake, swamp, slough, and sanctuary within a hundred miles. The clincher: *All buses leave at 5:00 a.m.* "In the middle of the night!" I wailed to a classmate. "We'll need miners' lamps."

I found the course mind-numbing. Who, I wondered, could possibly care that a Cooper's hawk and a sharp-shinned hawk are dead ringers for each other? Professor Myers cared passionately. Who cared that a Carolina wren has a white eyebrow stripe and sings *Tea kettle, tea kettle, tea kettle,* and an ordinary house wren has a muted eye ring and sings with a scratchy gargle? Professor Myers played a recording of its voice and tried to imitate it, falling just a thimble of Listerine flat.

He'd go to any length to transfuse his love of nature to his students. Illustrating the wing beat of a mallard, he flailed his short, stubby arms like a windmill in a hurricane. To remind us that the osprey usually builds elaborate nests high in trees or on top of poles, he hopped up on a chair and rendered its loud squawking song. And one day, trying to portray a kingfisher diving for a catch, he folded his hands in front of his face, ran across the room, kamikazied toward the wastebasket—then did a miraculous flyby and segued into the mating dance of whooping cranes.

When Professor Myers wasn't imitating birds, he was waxing poetic about them. "Their songs have inspired symphonies, their beauty sonnets," he declared. "And if you watch them for only a season, study them for only a semester, they will steal your heart away and give you a lifetime of enjoyment."

Drawing on his encyclopedic knowledge, he would constantly quiz us about things we came upon while moving through woods, marshes, and meadows. "What bird uses this plant to line its nests?" he would ask, pointing out a prickly thistle. Answer: a goldfinch likes thistledown. Or upon seeing a tree's bark perforated by the bill of a bird, he would want to know the name of the tree, the bird that turned it into a punchboard, and what the bird was drilling for.

Amazingly, I passed the course and graduated—finally packing away my bird guide and binoculars. The only good I seemed to get out of Professor Myers's course was a trove of stories about his antics and what I joked was "the most worthless class I ever took." My tales never failed to amuse friends and associates.

Then time brought marriage and kids and camping trips to the outdoors I had vowed to detour forever. With my family, I discovered a world I had missed before. Together we learned to identify plants, insects, fossils, flowers, stars, trees, and, yes, even birds. Professor Myers's lessons, cast away for years, returned like bread on water.

At a mountainside campsite, my wife, Shirley, our four children, and I were entertained one evening by an acrobatic bird vacuuming insects like an airborne sweeper. "It's an Acadian flycatcher," I told them, surprising even myself. The kids were impressed.

And once on a hiking foray in the South, when the children worried over a bird that seemed to be struggling along the ground with an injured wing, I explained, "She's not hurt. It's a mother killdeer trying to decoy us away from her nest." Eventually, I took my field guide and binoculars out of mothballs and put them in my knapsack.

In our travels around the country, I could differentiate between the scrub jays we saw in Florida and the Steller's jays we came upon in California—all because of birding with Professor Myers. Trips out of the country were enriched by sightings of caracaras in the Amazon, blue-footed boobies in the Galápagos Islands, and wading flamingos so numerous that they painted African lakes pink.

However, it was daily encounters with birds at our feeder and at the edge of our woods that convinced me of my debt to Everett Myers. One day a rufous-sided towhee showed up in the yard, and I scrambled to get my binoculars. As I focused on the beautiful tricolored bird, it began singing in three-note trills, and suddenly I recalled Professor Myers's description of its song, *Drink your tea,* and I was overcome with the urge to thank the man who prophetically said, "Birds will steal your heart away and give you a lifetime of enjoyment."

So I called my alma mater from my home in Princeton, New Jersey, to inquire about him. He had died, I learned, ten years earlier. Just before I hung up I asked: did he have any survivors? Yes, two daughters, one in Iowa and one in Maryland. *Call them,* an inner voice prompted. And I did.

"I wish I could thank your dad," I said, "but it took me a long time to appreciate him and what he taught me. So telling you is the best thing I can do. He showed me that the closer you look at the world, the more beauty and wonder you see."

He also helped me understand that nature has some important things to teach us if we pay attention. One day when I saw finches fighting over a place on my bird feeder, I squirmed to think I might resemble them vying with other commuters for a train seat. I vowed to be less finch-like. Another time when I observed a pair of Canada geese tending their goslings, I recalled how they mate for life, and I wondered what secrets they might share about long-run marriages—if we could only read their honking. Or more to the point, how I could be more caring in my own long-run marriage. Another day when I craned at migrating ducks flying in a cooperative V, I was reminded that helping others is the best way for all of us to achieve our destination. And I vowed to be less self-serving and reach out a little more to those around me.

"Do you see it?" I whisper to granddaughters Jessica and Ashley. "Yes," they answer. "What kind is it?"

"Let me get a closer look," I reply, raising my binoculars. Then I describe the little yellow bird with reddish-brown rivulets down its chest. "I'd say it's a warbler," I venture, "but we'll have to look it up." In a minute I find a picture of a male yellow warbler in my field guide and ask the girls if they think it looks like our colorful friend in the bush.

"That's it exactly!" exclaims Ashley. Jessica moves closer to this sunbeam on a branch. Unfrightened, he begins singing a one-on-one concert to her: *Sweet, sweet, sweet, I'm so sweet.*

The warm light filtering through the trees frames the two of them in a still portrait of beauty, the kind I suspect God snaps especially for parents and grandparents.

When the warbler moves on, so do we. Talking as we walk down the trail, we look for more feathered delights.

"Tell me, Grandpa," Ashley asks, taking my hand, "how do you know so much about birds?"

"I really know very little," I answer, "but most of what I do know I owe to a college teacher." Then I tell the girls about Professor Myers and "the most worthless class I ever took."

In January the sight of a single brown creeper is sufficient to brighten the day, and the twittering of half a dozen goldfinches is like the music of angels.

BRADFORD TORREY

THE WOLF OF COHO CREEK

BY
MORRIS HOMER ERWIN

One spring morning many years ago, I had been prospecting for gold along Coho Creek on southeastern Alaska's Kupreanof Island, and as I emerged from a forest of spruce and hemlock, I froze in my tracks. No more than 20 paces away in the flat muskeg was a huge, black Alaskan timber wolf—caught in one of Trapper George's traps.

Old George had died the previous week of a heart attack, so the wolf was lucky I had happened along. Yet now, confused and frightened at my approach, the wolf backed away, straining at the trap chain. Then I noticed something else: it was a female, and her teats were full of milk. Somewhere, there was a den of hungry pups waiting for their mother.

From her appearance, I guessed that she had been trapped only a few days. That meant her pups were probably still alive, surely no more than a few miles away. But I suspected that if I tried to release the wolf, she would turn aggressive and try to tear me to pieces.

So I decided to search for her pups instead and began to look for incoming tracks that might lead me to her den. Fortunately, there were still a few remaining patches of snow. After several moments, I spotted paw marks on a trail skirting the muskeg.

The tracks led a half-mile through the forest, then up a rock-strewn slope. I finally spotted the den at the base of an enormous spruce. There wasn't a sound inside. Wolf pups are shy and cautious, and I didn't have much hope of luring them outside. But I had to try. So I began imitating the high-pitched squeak of a mother wolf calling her young. No response.

A few moments later, after I tried another call, four tiny pups appeared. They couldn't have been more than a few weeks old. I extended my hands, and they tentatively suckled at my fingers. Perhaps hunger had helped overcome their natural fear. Then, one by one, I placed them in a burlap bag, and headed back down the slope.

When the mother wolf spotted me, she stood erect. Possibly picking up the scent of her young, she let out a high-pitched, plaintive whine. I released the pups, and they raced to her. Within seconds, they were slurping at her belly.

What next? I wondered. The mother wolf was clearly suffering. Yet each time I moved in her direction, a menacing growl rumbled in her throat. With her young to protect, she was becoming belligerent. *She needs nourishment,* I thought. *I have to find her something to eat.*

I hiked toward Coho Creek, and spotted the leg of a winter-killed deer sticking out of a snowbank. I cut off a hind quarter, then returned the remains to nature's icebox. Toting the venison haunch back to the wolf, I whispered in a soothing tone, "Okay, mother, your dinner is served. But only if you stop growling at me. C'mon now. Easy." I tossed chunks of venison in her direction. She sniffed them, then gobbled them up.

Cutting hemlock boughs, I fashioned a rough shelter for myself and was soon asleep. At dawn I was awakened by four fluffy bundles of fur sniffing at my face and hands. I glanced toward the agitated mother wolf. *If I could only win her confidence,* I thought. It was her only hope.

Over the next few days, I divided my time between prospecting and trying to win the wolf's trust. I talked gently with her, threw her more venison, and played with the pups. Little by little, I kept edging closer—though I was careful to remain beyond the length of her chain. The big animal never took her dark eyes off me. "Come on, mother," I pleaded. "You want to go back to your friends on the mountain. Relax."

At dusk on the fifth day, I delivered her daily fare of venison. "Here's dinner," I said softly as I approached. "C'mon, girl. Nothing to be afraid of." Suddenly, the pups came bounding to me. At least I had *their* trust. But I was beginning to lose hope of ever winning over the mother. Then I thought I saw a slight wagging of her tail. I moved within the length of her chain.

She remained motionless. My heart in my mouth, I sat down eight feet from her. One snap of her huge jaws and she could break my arm . . . or my neck. I wrapped my blanket around me and slowly settled onto the cold ground. It was a long time before I fell asleep.

I awoke at dawn, stirred by the sound of the pups nursing. Gently, I leaned over and petted them. The mother wolf stiffened. "Good morning, friends," I said tentatively. Then I slowly placed my hand on the wolf's injured leg. She flinched, but made no threatening move. *This can't be happening,* I thought. *Yet it is.*

I could see that the trap's steel jaws had imprisoned only two toes. They were swollen and lacerated, but she wouldn't lose the paw—if I could free her.

"Okay," I said. "Just a little longer and we'll have you out of there."

I applied pressure; the trap sprang open, and the wolf pulled free. Whimpering, she loped about, favoring the injured paw. My experience in the wild suggested the wolf would now gather her pups and vanish into the woods. But cautiously, she crept toward me.

The pups nipped playfully at their mother as she stopped at my elbow. Slowly, she sniffed my hands and arms. Then the wolf began licking my fingers. I was astonished. This went against everything I'd ever heard about timber wolves. Yet, strangely, it all seemed so natural.

After a while, with her pups scurrying around her, the mother wolf was ready to leave and began to limp off toward the forest. Then she turned back to me. "You want me to come with you, girl?" I asked. Curious, I packed my gear, and set off.

Following Coho Creek for a few miles, we ascended Kupreanof Mountain until we reached an alpine meadow. There, lurking in the forested perimeter, was a wolf pack—I counted nine adults and, judging by their playful antics, four nearly full-grown pups. After a few minutes of greeting, the pack broke into howling. It was an eerie sound, ranging from low wails to high-pitched yodeling.

At dark, I set up camp. By the light of my fire and a glistening moon, I could see furtive wolf shapes dodging in and out of the shadows, eyes shining. I had no fear. They were merely curious. So was I.

I awoke at first light. It was time to leave the wolf to her pack. She watched as I assembled my gear and started walking across the meadow. Reaching the far side, I looked back. The mother and her pups were sitting where I had left them, watching me. I don't know why, but I waved. At the same time, the mother wolf sent a long, mournful howl into the crisp air.

Four years later, after serving in World War II, I returned to Coho Creek in the fall of 1945. After the horrors of the war, it was good to be back among the soaring spruce and breathing the familiar, bracing air of the Alaskan bush. Then I saw, hanging in a red cedar where I had placed it four years before, the now-rusted steel trap that had ensnared the mother wolf. The sight of it gave me a strange feeling, and something made me climb Kupreanof Mountain to the meadow where I had last seen her. There, standing on a lofty ledge, I gave out a long, low wolf call—something I had done many times before.

An echo came back across the distance. Again I called. And again the echo reverberated, this time followed by a wolf call from a ridge about a half-mile away.

Then, far off, I saw a dark shape moving slowly in my direction. As it crossed the meadow, I could see it was a black timber wolf. A chill spread through my whole body. I knew at once that familiar shape, even after four years. "Hello, old girl," I called gently. The wolf edged closer, ears erect, body tense, and stopped a few yards off, her bushy tail wagging slightly.

Moments later, the wolf was gone. I left Kupreanof Island a short time after that, and I never saw the animal again. But the memory she left with me—vivid, haunting, a little eerie—will always be there, a reminder that there are things in nature that exist outside the laws and understanding of man.

During that brief instant in time, this injured animal and I had somehow penetrated each other's worlds, bridging barriers that were never meant to be bridged. There is no explaining experiences like this. We can only accept them and—because they're tinged with an air of mystery and strangeness—perhaps treasure them all the more.

You shall find a fuller satisfaction in the woods than in books. The trees and the rocks will teach you that which you cannot learn from masters.

SAINT BERNARD OF CLAIRVAUX

INCIDENT AT OSSABAW

BY
NASH MCINTOSH

You can still find pristine places off the Georgia coast between Savannah Beach and Ossabaw Sound—islands as wild as they were centuries ago. Those are the places I go whenever I can.

One such island had a huge osprey nest in a gnarled, windblown pine, and a fine broad beach. I knew that a three-day northeaster had deposited enormous amounts of white sand along the eastern shore, making it a perfect campsite. That's where we headed—six of us, good friends, three couples off on an overnight outing.

As my dory plied across Ossabaw Sound, there was among us a surge of anticipation that our expedition would be one of those golden moments when good friends enjoy one another's company without reservation—where time would slow almost to a full stop.

I heard something like a dog's bark, and turned leeward. There was a large bottlenose dolphin, clearing its blowhole not 30 feet off our beam. Others materialized behind him. They kept to the outer edge of our wake, first just the male, and then, looming up behind him, the rest of the pod—perhaps 20 dolphins in all.

Their fixed smiles are an accident, I know. But who could doubt their good nature? They streaked alongside like living outriggers, dorsal fins slicing effortlessly through the warm waters.

One succeeded the other, rolling and cavorting as if daring us to play with them on their terms. I resisted the temptation to ease the throttle forward, to pick up the challenge to race. I've tried that from time to time, only to learn anew that these ebullient creatures can easily spurt ahead of most boats merely by moving their wonderfully efficient tail flukes a bit faster.

There was no indication of anything unusual as the playful group gamboled along, keeping station with us. Then something changed. I sensed it before I could actually see what had happened. Something had interrupted the pod's flowing motion. Two dolphins—females, I assumed—had dropped back. I damped down the throttle and let the boat come about a bit so we could watch. One of the females was flexing her body in a taut arc, as if convulsed with pain, while the second nosed up against her.

As the distressed dolphin writhed in the water, we could see from her belly that she was at the point of giving birth. But what happened next was not to be visible to us. The pod abruptly submerged as if wanting to be unobserved during the moment of birth.

Having spent most of my life on the water, I've heard stories about how an expectant dolphin, still swimming, even at the peak of labor, occasionally arches her body, attended by at least one companion and encircled by the rest of the pod. At last there would be a small cloud of blood, and suddenly a fully-formed baby dolphin would appear.

Daylight was fading, so I started the engine again, and we left the scene, speeding across the two miles of open water to our island.

The great live oaks and palmettos that came down to the shoreline were heavily festooned with Spanish moss, and the rosy light of sunset cast a beautiful lavender glow over the beach. We had brought steaks and salad, and a tent large enough to sleep everyone. The weather forecast was for a mild evening and clear day to come.

That proved all wrong. Soon the skies darkened, and flashes of lightning signaled an approaching storm. We hurried about the task of putting up the tent. Three people stood inside, with fabric drooping all over them. Three others were outside with eight pieces of tent framework in hand. There were guylines and pegs, which we learned weren't suited for use on a beach.

We laughed as we realized how inept we were at setting up a complicated new tent in a gale. But at last, in the pelting rain, we succeeded, even if the tent did not remotely resemble the trim tautness displayed in the mail-order catalog.

We retreated inside, thoroughly drenched. As leader of the expedition and chef, it was my job to cook. After 40 minutes, the steaks were ready. From the sound of crunching, I could tell that sand had permeated everything.

We got through it somehow, laughing at the strange turn our idyllic outing had taken. Finally, cold and exhausted, we turned in.

During the wee hours, there was a thunderous crash as the boat, driven by an onshore wind, waves, and the rising tide, came sailing through the side of the tent, just missing three of us and causing the tent to collapse.

At breakfast, my mood and the inner weather of our whole group were as dark as the scudding clouds. We broke camp before nine and headed back home across the broad reach of water. I rebuffed several attempts to chat me out of the dumps. Annoyed and even bitter, I wondered why life at times seems to have more downs than ups.

As we headed north, a group of dolphins—was it the same one?—surfaced a few points off our port bow. The others saw them, too, and there was murmuring of a sort that let me know they'd seen something that had escaped me.

As the boat came abeam of the pod, I recognized the large male that had suddenly appeared at our side the day before. And I could also see the baby dolphin, being pushed by its mother, just behind the male. But the newborn was not animated. In fact it did not move at all. It was dead, and we campers, so full of regret for our blighted holiday, of annoyance over drenched clothing and loss of comfort for a short time, suddenly knew how flimsy were our sorrows compared with what we saw now. Surrounding the bereaved mother were the other members of the pod, defending her from any shark that might be tempted to come close.

I killed the motor. We all looked silently at this stately cortege, living evidence of unconditional commitment of one dolphin to another.

It almost seemed to me as if the dead newborn was being carried to deep water, for burial at sea. I removed my hat, unconsciously, as the procession veered away from us and through the tidal creek, past the old lighthouse and out to Ossabaw Sound.

As I watched them go, I realized that we in the boat were all one again. Our petty annoyance had departed, and the feeling of amity and mutual regard was back, intact, unaffected now by the travails of the night. I knew all this though not a word was said.

As I turned to restart the motor, a shaft of the morning sun cut through the departing clouds and illuminated for the last time the low forms swimming on the far side of the sound. In another few moments, they would be out to open sea.

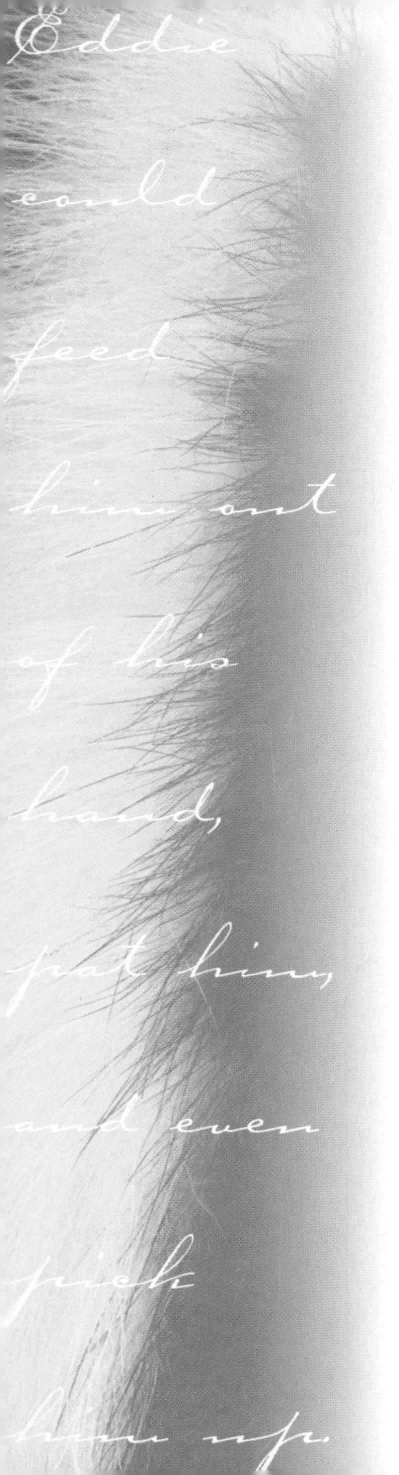

GREAT SKUNK CAPER

BY
BOB NOONAN

That summer vacation before high school started, I was broke. I tried picking peas at a local farm for a day, and made enough money to buy enough candy to give me enough energy to pick more peas.

My buddy Eddie was in the same boat. One afternoon we sat on the porch of the nursing home his mother owned, racking our brains for ways to make money. Eddie thumbed through a magazine and showed me an ad proclaiming in bold letters: "SKUNKS MAKE WONDERFUL PETS!" For a mere $50, it said, we could own a deodorized skunk.

The nursing home had a garbage dump out back, and we saw skunks there. They were attractive animals, and the thought of bothering them never crossed our minds. But $50! We would sell skunks for pets and become wealthy.

We agreed that deodorizing a skunk couldn't be too complicated. I'd taken a mail-order taxidermy course, and having stuffed a rat, pigeons, and a squirrel or two, I was sure I could handle the operation. We sent away for a booklet describing the procedure.

The next item we needed was a skunk. We had a dumpful—but how to lay our hands on one safely? Several local outdoorsmen were fond of telling us kids that if you grabbed an unsuspecting skunk by the tail and lifted his hind legs off the ground, he couldn't spray. It sounded scientific, but we were dubious. We decided we had to do more research.

We visited a local trapper, a man who supposedly released unwanted skunks from his traps—by hand. By the faint odor about him we knew he had an acquaintance with the species. He was a fountain of information.

"A skunk has two stink glands on his behind," he told us. "He sprays by squeezing muscles around the glands, aiming for the face when possible. He can score a direct hit out to twelve feet. The stuff ejects in yellow drops, then expands into a mist. It'll choke and blind you for a minute, but it won't really hurt you.

"A skunk is a peaceful animal and won't spray unless provoked," he continued. "But he'll give warnings first. If you get too close, he'll stop what he's doing and raise his tail. If you keep coming, he'll point his rear end at you and look over his shoulder, taking aim. If you're still coming, he'll raise the tip of his tail. That's a bad sign. When you see that, take a deep breath, cover your eyes, and hit the deck. He's gonna shoot.

"When I catch a skunk in a trap, I approach real slow and talk to it quiet. A calm voice can keep it from getting riled. I keep moving until the tail goes up. I stop, keep talking, and pretty soon the tail goes down and I move in again."

We digested this information. Then Eddie asked, "If you grab a skunk by the tail and lift his hind legs off the ground, can he still spray?"

"Don't know," said the trapper. "Never tried."

The how-to booklet arrived a few days later. We memorized the instructions and set up an operating table in the barn. We located a spray can of ether, and made a cone of stiff paper. The booklet told us

to spray the ether into some cotton balls positioned in the bottom of the cone, and insert the skunk's head into the cone until he was anesthetized and passed out. Now we were ready to grab a skunk.

Eddie volunteered. Just before sundown we reached the dump, and skunks appeared to our left. In the lead was a mother, big as a watermelon, nose to ground, tail half-erect. Behind her came three smaller, leaner editions of herself. They went directly to the 15-foot-high wall of trash, broke up, and started individual inspection of the goodies.

We tensed. One youngster was working his way in our direction. When he was 25 feet away, Eddie moved in. When he was ten feet away, the skunk turned and peered at Eddie. He hoisted his tail a bit—just like the trapper said he would.

Eddie froze. Then, talking in a low monotone, he soothed the skunk. "Boy are you gonna love being a pet—all you can eat—fish, candy bars, steak, french fries, ice cream . . ." He droned on, promising skunk bliss.

The trapper proved right again. The skunk lowered his tail and stuck his head into a peanut-butter jar. But as Eddie moved forward, the skunk got nervous and raised his tail. Eddie stopped and talked, and the skunk continued supper. Eddie shuffled to within five feet of the skunk, who walked off—not alarmed, but not about to let Eddie get too close.

Eddie saw an old refrigerator and started to herd the skunk toward it. I saw his plan immediately. The skunk became trapped against the refrigerator and the wall of trash. Agitated, he hoisted his tail. Eddie froze again—and I held my breath.

Then from behind a sofa came disaster. Momma had realized junior was missing and was hunting for him—heading straight for Eddie's backside. "Eddie," I hissed in a stage whisper. "Behind you."

Eddie turned. "Quiet," he replied. "I've almost got him."

Only a few feet away, momma raised her tail. I yelled again, "Eddie! Behind you!" Eddie swiveled and saw momma. In his panic he moved too fast—a big mistake.

The trapper was right again. With the wisdom born of thousands of years of skunk evolution, momma whipped her rear end around and squirted Eddie right between the lookers.

Poor Eddie! He let out a screech that must've lifted the old-timers out of their chairs at the nursing home. Clawing at his face, he took off, thereby making another mistake. He'd forgotten about junior, who let fly too. Wailing, Eddie crashed into a nearby swamp. I followed him, running into a solid, tangible wall of stink. I gasped, staggered, and forged ahead, choking.

I found Eddie 20 feet away rolling on the ground and splashing mud, leaves, and swamp water on his face. "Are you all right?" I asked.

"Fine!" he gasped, whereupon we both burst into hysterical laughter.

On the way home, both Eddie and I agreed the smell wasn't objectionable at all. In fact, close contact with the odor had overwhelmed our noses, rendering them temporarily useless. However, others at home had not been desensitized. We were forced to strip in the backyard, and the hose was turned on us. We slept in the barn that night.

Our next move was to build a box trap, a beauty with a sliding door held up by a stick tied to a string that went through a hole in the rear of the trap and was tied to a dead mouse. When the skunk pulled on the string, he'd pull out the stick holding the door open. It worked great—and within a day we had our skunk.

Eddie spent more time with the skunk than I did. Whenever I came near, the skunk grew nervous, but Eddie could feed him out of his hand, pat him, and even pick him up.

Operation day had arrived. Eddie would hold the skunk while I loaded the ether cone, then position the cone near the skunk's face till he got woozy. When he was out cold, I'd operate.

We approached quietly. I stayed behind Eddie, out of sight. He reached in, grabbed him across the back, and stood up. The tail, hind legs, and firing mechanism hung free, out of reach of the ground—the skunk didn't spray! Now we could tell the trapper a thing or two.

We headed for the barn. Until now, the skunk had no idea there was anyone there but him and Eddie. Then the skunk saw me, bared his needle-like teeth, and bit Eddie's thumb.

Eddie bellowed in pain and let go. The skunk fell to the ground. Eddie was too high for a good face shot, so the skunk gave him a blast to the legs. I turned and got a few feet away, but the skunk dosed me on my back. Staggering away, I got hit again. Then I turned to see the skunk give Eddie a final shot—feebler than the others. He was running out of scent and must have known it because he headed for the woods at a fast skunk shuffle.

A little madness in the spring is wholesome even for the king.

EMILY DICKINSON

Visions of peas entered my mind as I saw the $50 bill beelining for freedom. We hadn't gone this far, through this much, to see our plans foiled. I had nothing to lose. I took after him at a dead run and nabbed him by the tail. Suspended in the air, both guns empty, he was ours.

Eddie held the ether cone close to the skunk's face, and soon he was asleep on the operating table. I proceeded carefully, the booklet open beside me. In 20 minutes the skunk was back in his pen minus his artillery. The anesthesiologist and surgeon shook hands, mightily pleased with themselves. Even the hose and banishment to the barn again did not dampen our contentment.

We never did sell the skunk, though. Eddie got attached to him and named him Jake. He lived with Eddie for the rest of the year and was a favorite of the nursing-home residents. Everyone loved the calm, good-natured, dignified little animal. Spoiled and fed constantly, he grew to blimplike proportions. It was great entertainment to see Jake flow downstairs like a fur-covered water balloon. He had truly gone to skunk heaven.

Eddie and I successfully trapped and deodorized a few more skunks and sold them. We never got $50—but at least we never had to pick peas again. Maybe that's why, to this day, the smell of skunk is attractive to me—a rich, pungent, satisfying odor.

ONE HOT AFTERNOON IN JULY

BY
RALPH KINNEY BENNETT

There are certain days when we feel our lives change profoundly, days we remember for a lifetime. Such, for me, was one afternoon in July in the Ligonier Valley of Pennsylvania, at a place called Devil's Hole.

It happened in that timeless time before school imposed the first real framework on life. The summer sky was bluer then, the sycamores smiled in the sun, and the hot days drowsed by, punctuated with velvet evenings when fireflies flashed outside my bedroom window.

On that morning my twin brother, Roger, and I had finished our chores, and the whole day lay before us. "Let's go to Devil's Hole," Roger suggested.

I readily agreed, but for all my eagerness there was a leaden feeling deep in my stomach. Although he had never said a word about it, never taunted me, Roger could swim and I could not. Earlier in the summer he had slid eagerly off the outstretched hands of our older brother, Richard, thrashed his feet and arms, and propelled himself through the water. I had been too afraid or embarrassed to try. Now Roger could slip through the water expertly, and he moved, it seemed to me, on a different plane—with the experienced, confident older kids.

Roger led the way back to the kitchen door. "Grandma, can we go to Devil's Hole?" We leaned against the screen, peering into the dark kitchen. Grandma, busy mixing the batter for spice cakes, stood at the kitchen counter, a bright speckle of sunlight and apple tree leaves reflected in her glasses. "Well, I guess the big kids are up there now, but mind the road," she admonished with a flourish of her wooden spoon, "and be careful in that place."

With a yell, Roger threw open the screen door, tore through the kitchen, and scrambled up the stairs. I followed, racing to get into my Sears, Roebuck bathing suit. Slinging towels around our necks, we loped across the field next to our house, and headed up the dirt road.

Had I been asked then to define fun and freedom, it would have been in terms of a boy swimming fearlessly through the water. It was delight and danger all at once.

The danger was no small thing. My acquaintance with the mystery of death was brief but vivid. A neighborhood dog had been hit by a car; it lay with its teeth showing and one eye staring up at the sky. Then there were the times Mom would point her finger at dark headlines in the Latrobe *Bulletin* and explain this terrible thing called drowning, which had befallen someone swimming at Kingston Dam or some other nearby pond or stream.

Roger and I reached Linn Run. There, at a place where sunlight flooded through a break in the trees, a slight slope of smoothly rounded pebbles and mossy ground led to a deep green pool of icy water reflecting two huge, partially submerged boulders on the opposite bank.

As far back as anyone could remember, the place had been called Devil's Hole. Indians must have swum there long before the British and the French fought each other in these mountains. Deer still came there

at night to drink. In the spring the older boys performed the annual ritual of piling rocks the size of basketballs across the creek until the water began to rise, inch by inch, up the gray boulders.

This dam was my province and protection. While the others swam, I always pretended to be intent upon minor repairs to it, or trying to catch minnows along its base with an old tin can.

When we first arrived, I watched enviously as Roger joined the older boys and girls. They nonchalantly dived in, swam swiftly across the pool, and pulled themselves up on the big rocks to luxuriate in the sun. Among them was Nancy Storer, sitting on the closer boulder in a white one-piece bathing suit with tiny blue polka dots. She baby-sat for us occasionally, and I adored her. She watched as boys began cannonballing off the lower boulder, their shouts and splashes and laughter echoing through the trees.

Quietly I ventured in. Feeling the shock of the cold water, I carefully planted my toes on the smooth and slippery round rocks of the bottom. With the dam as a handrail, I made my way to the middle of the creek. Behind me, someone on the rocks was whooping like Tarzan.

More than ever I wanted to be a part of that fun. I turned from the security of the dam and waded a few feet upstream. The scene before me is still frozen in memory like a photograph—kids jumping, diving, playing tag as tiny rainbows arced through splashing water.

Now the water was up almost to my chest. I held my arms out in front of me, my hands clasped tightly, shivering from the coldness.

Suddenly there was nothing under my feet. I plunged beneath the surface.

For an instant I comprehended a liquid shaft of sunlight, a corner of the gray boulder disappearing into the gravel and rocks of the bottom, and somewhere ahead of me a pair of white legs treading water beneath a cloud of sparkling bubbles. Eerie, muffled laughter and shouts came from somewhere above me.

For that frozen second I felt myself in a strange new world. Then came a mad kaleidoscope of watery light and darkness—thrashing, spluttering, gurgling—a feeling of utter terror in my bursting chest. For a fraction of a second, I saw sun-dappled leaves in the trees far above me and heard voices clearly. Then I was back in a white hail of bubbles, and a roaring filled my ears. I saw that dead dog's staring eye.

I kicked my legs; my arms thrashed forward; my face came out of the water and I gulped air. Yelling "whoah, whoah," I was wrestling with water and fear in a crazy scramble of arms and legs.

August is nature's nap.

BERN WILLIAMS

But I was moving through the water! In an exquisite instant I felt terror turn to exhilaration. I was swimming.

I did not turn for the bank of the creek and safety. I headed into the deep green at the center of Devil's Hole—toward those unreachable boulders. Roger was standing on the bigger boulder, his mouth a perfect O as he watched me.

But my eyes were fixed on Nancy. There was a half-smile on her freckled face as my madly kicking, churning progress drew me closer.

I touched the boulder on which she sat. I held on, treading water, breathing in great ragged gulps and feeling indescribably triumphant.

"Well, hello," she said, looking down at me, almost laughing the words.

I felt totally exhausted for a moment. But I did not want to leave the water. I was afraid I would forget how to do what I had done. I pushed off from the rock and quickly thrashed around in a circle, then grabbed the rock again. I could scarcely believe it. I wanted to shout, "I can swim!" but the presence of my brother and the other boys was enough to prevent it.

I felt glorious. Unstoppable. I splashed across the stream to the bank by the road, touched bottom with my feet, then swam back into the middle again.

The sun was playing hide-and-seek in the tops of the trees by the time I said good-bye to Nancy and the other kids. I felt much bigger and taller than I had ever felt before. Roger and I started down the dirt road for home, our damp towels hanging behind us like limp capes. I felt the hot sun on my wet hair. I could smell the fresh, wonderful scent of Devil's Hole, the water, the moss, the laurel.

We were almost to the Critchfields' house before Roger said, "It's pretty easy, huh . . . swimming."

"Yep," I answered, recognizing the immense accolade I had just received from my twin.

I skipped the rest of the way home. Grandma was starting to cook dinner. Mom wasn't home from work yet.

"Grandma, I swam today!" I shouted.

She looked up from the stove, a dark alarm in her face. "What? Did one of those hoodlums throw you in?"

"No, Grandma. I just did it. I just up and did it."

I swaggered around the yard a bit, keeping to myself, reliving every moment in the water that day. After dinner we played prisoner's base with the neighborhood kids as the shadows lengthened. Then we all got out our coffee cans and Mason jars to catch lightning bugs.

But the call finally came: "Come on in, kids—time for bed." More tired than I thought I was, I said my prayers with Mom and Roger and settled under the covers. With my face close to the screened window, I lay in the darkness, listening to the sounds of summer: the ripple of the creek, the loud whir and chirp of cicadas and tree frogs.

I didn't fully comprehend it then, but I had learned something very important: the dark barrier called fear may be high and imposing, but it is often exceedingly thin. It appears again and again throughout our lives. Sometimes a touch breaks through it; sometimes, in the desperate need of the moment, we must put our shoulder to it like a fireman breaking down a door. And sometimes our very yearning makes it fall.

My eyes grew heavy. I imagined myself smoothly parting cool waters, swimming expertly, quietly, sleekly—not only at Devil's Hole but in great rivers, in the mighty ocean.

A BOY AND HIS CAT

BY
JUDITH S. JOHNESSEE

I'm not sure how he got to my clinic. He didn't look old enough to drive, although his child's body had begun to broaden and he moved with the heavy grace of young manhood. His face was direct and open.

When I walked into the waiting room, he was lovingly petting his cat through the open door of the carrier on his lap. With a schoolboy's faith in authority, he had brought his sick cat in for me to mend.

The cat was a tiny thing, exquisitely formed, with a delicate skull and beautiful markings. She was about the boy's own age, give or take a year. I could see how her spots and stripes and her fierce, bright face had evoked the image of a tiger in a child's mind, and Tigress she had become.

Age had dimmed the bright green fire of her eyes into faded lace, but she was still elegant and self-possessed. She greeted me with a friendly rub against my hand.

I began to ask questions to determine what had brought this charming pair to see me. Unlike most adults, the boy answered simply and directly. Tigress had had a normal appetite until recently, when she'd begun to vomit a couple of times a day. Now she was not eating at all and had withdrawn from her human family. She had also lost a pound, which is a lot when you weigh only six.

Stroking Tigress, I told her how beautiful she was while I examined her eyes and mouth, listened to her heart and lungs, and felt her stomach. My fingers found it: a tubular mass in mid-abdomen. Tigress politely tried to slip away. She did not like the mass being handled.

I looked at the fresh-faced boy and back at the cat he had probably had all his life. I was going to have to tell him that his beloved companion had a tumor. Even if it were surgically removed, she probably would survive less than a year, and might need weekly chemotherapy to last that long.

It would all be very difficult and expensive. So I was going to have to tell this boy that his cat was likely to die. And there he was, all alone.

Death is something we push to the background and ignore as long as possible, but in reality every living thing we love will die. It is an omnipresent part of life. How death is first experienced can be life-forming. It can be a thing of horror and suffering, or a peaceful release.

So I would have to guide the boy through this myself. I did not want the burden. It had to be done perfectly, or he might end up emotionally scarred.

It would have been easy to shirk this task and summon a parent. But when I looked at the boy's face, I could not do it. He knew something was wrong. I could not just ignore him. So I talked to him as Tigress's rightful owner and told him as gently as I could what I had found, and what it meant.

As I spoke, the boy jerked convulsively away from me, probably so I could not see his face, but I had seen it begin to twist as he turned. I sat down and turned to Tigress, to give the boy some privacy, and

stroked her beautiful old face while I discussed the alternatives with him: I could do a biopsy of the mass, let her fade away at home, or give her an injection and put her to sleep.

He listened carefully and nodded gravely. He said he didn't think she was very comfortable anymore, and he didn't want her to suffer. He was trying very hard. The pair of them broke my heart. I offered to call a parent to explain what was going on.

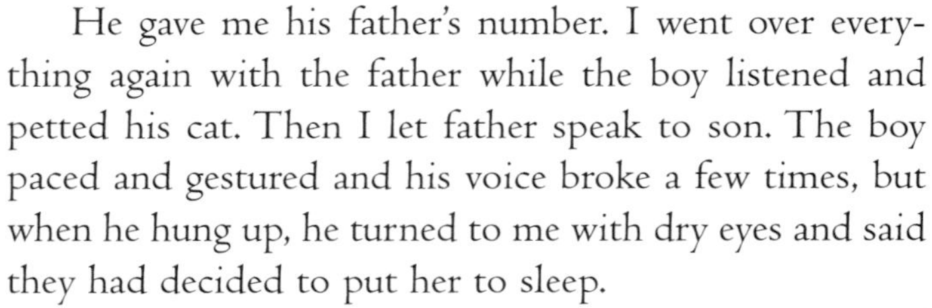

He gave me his father's number. I went over everything again with the father while the boy listened and petted his cat. Then I let father speak to son. The boy paced and gestured and his voice broke a few times, but when he hung up, he turned to me with dry eyes and said they had decided to put her to sleep.

No rage, no denial, no hysteria, just acceptance of the inevitable. I could see, though, how much it was costing him. I asked if he wanted to take her home overnight to say good-bye. But he said no. He just wanted to be alone with her for a few minutes.

I left them and went to sign out the barbiturate I would use to ease her into a painless sleep. I could not control the tears streaming down my face, or the grief I felt welling inside for this boy who had had to become a man so quickly and so alone.

I waited outside the exam room. In a few minutes he came out and said that he was ready. I asked if he wanted to stay with her. He looked surprised, but I explained that it was often easier to observe how peaceful it was than forever to wonder how it actually happened.

Immediately seeing the logic of that, he held her head and reassured her while I administered the injection. She drifted off to sleep, her head cradled in his hand.

The animal looked quiet and at rest. The owner now bore all the suffering. This was the finest gift you could give, I said, to assume another's pain so that a loved one might rest.

He nodded. He understood.

Something was missing, though. I did not feel I had completed my task. It came to me suddenly that though I had asked him to become a man instantly, and he had done so with grace and strength, he was still a child.

I held out my arms and asked him if he needed a hug. He did indeed, and in truth, so did I.

God made the beauties of nature like a child playing in the sand.

APOLLONIUS OF TYANA

An INVITATION *to* ADVENTURE

Special Feature

BY
JAMES McCRACKEN

My wife Betty and I walk across the road from our camp. Only 20 feet from our tent to the road, and another 30 feet to the lake. We stand, hand in hand. The sun is setting. Small waves, with white tops like the teeth of a silver saw, rush toward us, then crumble on the sands at our feet. Sebago Lake, in the southwestern corner of Maine, lies south of us, and a chill fall wind rides over the waves, driving them to destruction on our northern shore.

Betty buttons the top button of her jacket. The sun has gone. The day is done. We turn and walk through the heavy sand to our camp. As we reach the road we meet a young couple, out for a walk. They look at us, look at our tent.

"You're camping?" the young man asks.

"Yes, camping and canoeing."

We cross the road. The tent flaps are open to the evening air. Our sleeping bags lie on the ground like long woolly bears who have found shelter against the bitter winter to come.

"We're four campsites up from here," the young man says. He sends a look toward out tent. "You have air mattresses, don't you?"

I explain to him that our son *did* have air mattresses, and he intended for us to have them. But they leaked.

The girl smiles. "Y'know, I'll bet my own parents aren't as old as you two are. But they wouldn't be caught dead here. Sleeping on the ground, cooking out." She turns to our bright yellow canoe, pulled up into the white pine on the other side of the road. "And you canoe, too?"

We say that we do. Most of every day.

"Look," the young man blurts, "we have air mattresses. They make a big difference, but we don't need 'em." He looks at the girl. "Do we?"

She smiles again. "No way. Why don't you take them?"

Strangers in the night. They offer us comfort. We really don't need them, we say. But we're grateful for the offer.

They turn toward their own campsite. "You two, you're something else," the young man says. They wave, and walk off down the road.

We stand, hand in hand, our minds savoring the days just passed.

My wife's hair was blond, a tawny blond with a lighter streak in the middle, running back from her forehead. The light streak was hardly noticeable in the winter, but in the summer it seemed to leap to life, adding to her attractiveness. These days her hair, while still light, is salted with gray. And it isn't long to her shoulders the way it used to be. Now her hair is neatly trimmed, and the tawny blond, the color of youth, is fading.

Fortunately the human spirit need not fade. In his book *The Spectator Bird,* Wallace Stegner tells of a letter from eighty-five-year-old author Bruce Bliven. Bliven wrote that when asked if he feels like an old man, he replies that he does not. He feels like a young man with something the matter with him. That is the human spirit at its strongest. Unfading, unwrinkled. That is the spirit of the tawny-haired girl, my wife.

I retired in the springtime. It was wonderful. There was grass to be fertilized, then mowed. There was the garden to be planted.

Betty and I got to know each other again. There was time to chat, to reminisce, to look ahead. But summer passed; autumn came and drained into winter. And then another spring. Ah, another spring.

Once more the garden was planted, the grass fertilized and mowed. There was an occasional game of golf. But we'd been through this before. Was there nothing more now than mowing grass, tending the garden, reading, and talking? Was this what retirement came to?

In the late afternoon or early evening we would get into the car and drive to the river. Our river, the Connecticut, harbors many craft, great and small. Our town dock at Essex is more parking area than dock. It is paved with broken asphalt. There is room for perhaps a dozen cars along the waterfront. People sit and stare out at the boats and the river. It reminds one of the old folks who used to sit on verandas of summer hotels. A distant, almost vacant look comes to the eyes. They are thinking, perhaps, of days gone by when they sailed boats like these moored before them.

We watched a sloop head downriver with the current and tide. It was bound—where? Block Island, Nantucket, Martha's Vineyard, Maine? We were bound for home. The romance of setting out for distant shores was not for us.

"Let's buy a boat," Betty said suddenly. I had just reached for the ignition switch. I paused. She had been dreaming, too.

A 30-footer? Fiberglas: $30,000. Perhaps more. Well, why not? If not a sailboat, we could buy a power cruiser. Sixty thousand, with radar, radio direction finder, depth sounder, ship-to-shore radio, refrigerator, hot and cold running water. Why not? Why not freedom for us, too? I thought of our Social Security check. My pension. Well, we wouldn't need luxury. We might be able to pick up something for only $10,000. We could take a second mortgage on the house, pay it off, say, at $50 a month for the next 110 years.

I reached for the ignition switch again. Let's go home. Enough of this.

"No, wait," Betty said. She reached down beside her on the car seat and pulled out a catalogue. It seemed to open to a certain page where she had been before.

"Look!" she said. The book was open to a page describing canoes. Canoes?

Now I stared at her. "I don't get it."

"But why not buy a canoe?" She said it very slowly, then waited.

A picture came to mind. People go "white-water" canoeing, risking their bones, their lives, rushing over rocks and ragged boulders. Or they go romancing on a placid pond with the moon casting pewter pathways on the quiet waters. Canoeing, like most things today, is for the young.

We went home and talked about it. A year and a half before, I had suffered a heart attack. One doctor told me to exercise only moderately. Another told me to jog a bit. Another said *never* jog. Lawn mowing was okay, if I rested frequently.

So the decision came down, in essence, to me. Paddling a canoe should be mild enough exercise, but we could see circumstances when it might be strenuous. Presumably, there would be times of emergency. We decided that if we were to buy a canoe we would limit our voyages to mild shoreline excursions. What began as only a half-serious suggestion by my wife became a serious decision. We would buy a canoe.

The bright yellow craft sat beside our garage for four days before we gathered courage to hoist it atop our car. (This was not an easy feat for two aging people, one with an arthritic knee and the other with an arthritic shoulder.) Then we set out for the river, and the launching performance.

We were self-conscious and apprehensive. Perhaps one of us would find the task too much, and the canoe would crash to the ground. There were observers, of course, the usual dreamers at the waterfront. Perhaps they would think us old hands at this sort of thing. Perhaps they were waiting for some ridiculous development. Heave! Betty's knees buckled. My face turned purple under the strain. But we did it. The canoe was afloat.

We started off, both paddling on the same side. That was wrong. We crashed head-on into the handiest piling. The craft then began to drift under the boardwalk that the piling supported. Betty, in the bow, faced decapitation. We managed to reverse gears at the last moment. Someone on shore laughed.

Now, who paddles on which side? We decided, avoided the boardwalk, and slid out into the river. Ah, this was it! Now we were canoeing. The current caught us, and we began to move out toward the middle. That wasn't quite what we had in mind. The current was carrying us inexorably downstream. We soon found ourselves out where the river wanted us, in the shipping channel.

The channel is where the big boats travel: oil tankers laden with fuel for East Hartford, cruise ships bound for Block Island and Martha's Vineyard, sailing vessels. And now, us.

There we were. The tide was falling, and the river current was rushing toward Long Island Sound. Suddenly we saw that Essex was half a mile upstream. How did it get there so fast? We rested a moment to discuss the situation. Paddle for shore, we agreed, then back upstream. The canoe turned broadside, and that was our first opportunity to glance up the river. Beautiful sight? Terrifying sight!

There, not 200 yards away, was a yacht that looked like a white mountain bearing down on us at express-train speed.

"Paddle for your life!" I shouted.

We proceeded to do so, once more both stroking on the same side. Our vessel answered the challenge and aimed her bow straight toward the onbearing monster. The ship delivered an angry blast on her horn.

"Yessir, boss. *Yessir!*"

I shifted my paddle over to the other side. Betty did, too. So here we were cutting circles in the water again.

We held a calm, quiet, despairing council. Each of us yelling, "Paddle on the other side, you idiot!" End of council.

Shoulders aching, eyes bulging, faces drained of blood, we headed for—Essex? Hartford? St. Louis? Any place safe.

I ventured a glance over my shoulder. The ship was now 100 yards upstream and closing fast. Behind her she trailed a wake that would make a surfboarder envious. If we weren't run down, we would be swamped. End of the idyllic life and a canoe.

At that precise moment, the throb of the yacht's engines lowered to a muttering rumble. We looked around. The great white wave at her bow became a ribbon of lace. The comber she dragged behind rushed shoreward, but safely upstream from us.

The monster had assumed a canoe's pace. A man in a glass house up front waved to us. With an effort I raised my hand in thanks. Fifty yards downstream from us, the yacht's engines once more rumbled to life.

Our first venture out on the briny deep of the Connecticut River. And our first lesson in the innate courtesy of boating people. But, oh boy! That placid-looking, beguiling strip of blue water could be a trap!

We sat at home and thought things over. As far as I could detect, my heart had never skipped a beat during our race to safety. So we went out again. This time we stayed close to shore and paddled on opposite sides of the canoe. If I felt the slightest twinge of pain or ache in my left arm or pressure building in my chest, we stopped and drifted. It became easy and profoundly enjoyable.

Soon we learned that the tides of Long Island Sound exert enormous power over the river. So much, in fact, that the current reverses direction every six hours or so. I learned to read tide tables. We went down the river with the current, up with the tide. As time passed, I could paddle for longer and longer periods without discomfort. Paddling is marvelous exercise for back, shoulder, arm, even leg muscles.

We explored Hamburg Cove to its shallowest point. We paddled the Black Hall River, Selden Creek, Salmon River. Into nooks and crannies of coves and backwaters no power-boat could manage. We traversed marshlands, examining the surrounding flora, sometimes startling birds into protesting flight. We ate our lunches on small, sandy beaches and swam in warm, placid waters. Here, lying close by our doorstep, were adventures we might never have known. Our skins browned in the sun. Rolls of flesh at our middles melted away. We lost pounds—and gained a world.

Two or three times, as we traveled about by car, we had noticed a short, steep dirt road running off the highway. It led to a narrow stream, perhaps 75 feet wide. We purchased a navigation chart of the mouth of the Connecticut and identified the stream: the Lieutenant River. A day later, we launched the canoe at the bottom of the dirt road, and took off downstream with the outgoing tide. The Lieutenant is lined on both sides with marsh grass, tall and green. The water was dark, opaque; the marsh grass was the green of the sea. In a strong breeze it even looked like the sea, for the grass would bend to the wind in waves; great rollers without whitecaps.

Small birds hurried along the mud banks of the river. Spotted here and there were larger birds, pure white, with long, arching necks—snowy egrets. At a place where the water widens to form a pond we discovered a family of swans. Seagulls flew overhead. Fish swam beneath. Small animals ran among the sea-green reeds and grass.

Except for an occasional outboard engine, all was quiet. It was as though the world had receded to another place, another planet, with its noise and rush, anguish, anger, and pollution. We heard only the dip of our paddles in the quiet water.

I sat in the stern. Ahead was the lithe, brown back of my wife. Dip and stroke. Dip and stroke. My mind wandered back over the years. When we were married our ages combined totaled 45 years. Now they totaled 131. Years and years together. Good times and bad times. Sickness and health. All these things and more, experienced together. Our children grown and gone. Here we were, canoeing on a small river that led to another one, the Connecticut, that led to the sea. The sea. Yes, that distant mysterious place that lies ahead. But for now we are together, paddling down a placid stream.

One day, near the edge of the pond that shelters the swans, we were privy to one of nature's savage life-and-death struggles. A seagull was pecking and jabbing with such fury that it stirred up a miniature maelstrom in the water. Our paddles stopped in midair, small droplets peeling off and falling back to their source. Suddenly the gull rose from the surface; in its beak, whipping and lashing the air, was a snake or an eel. The gull tried to fly, but was thrown off balance by the victim's struggles. Back on the water, the gull renewed the battle, darting, pecking dauntlessly. Betty and I sat spellbound. We hoped the snake or eel might escape. But then—how does one weigh such things?

At last the struggle ebbed. The gull sat for a moment, gathering strength. One last lunge, then it rose from the water with the creature hanging lifelessly from its beak. Victory was the gull's, and it flew away. A life lost. Another prolonged.

Summer passed. July turned to August, August to September. The sun's rays lost their fierce heat. Accordingly, the water cooled. What had been long, languid swims were now quick dips. For most, no doubt, the coming of fall is a time of quickened step, of eager anticipation. For us it was not. It meant the approach of the day when we would have to store the canoe away. Bring in the outdoor furniture. Put away the hoe and rake, lawn mower and weeder. Secure storm windows.

But there was still time. The canoe gleamed bright yellow on top of the car, challenging and inviting. In the evenings we sat and talked about it. Could we? Should we? One week spent camping and canoeing? We could borrow the equipment—tent, sleeping bags, cooking utensils—from our son. It would cost very little, just the gasoline to get us there, wherever "there" was. We dug out maps. We purchased the Appalachian Mountain Club New England Canoeing Guide. The conversation would ebb and flow with our moods. Enthusiasm one moment, mistrust of our capabilities the next.

There was one overriding consideration: my heart. What if we were out in the middle of a lake or paddling down a remote river? Once I had asked a doctor about the chances of suffering another heart attack—this one crippling, or fatal. He had shrugged his shoulders. "Well," he answered, "there's only one way I can answer that. Your chances of another attack are greater than if you'd not suffered the first one. The elements are still there. We cannot remove them."

On such a trip, the nearest doctor could be five to ten hours away by canoe and car. Betty was willing, eager to go. But her wishes were subservient to reality. We knew that if I consulted my doctor he would urge caution, and that would dictate staying home. There was only one answer, the answer I would have to make. So it ended up with a rationalization. *My heart will beat until I die.* That is true of me; it is true of us all. Another attack could come while I sleep or drive my car. So why deny ourselves simple pleasures, the things we consider reasonable challenges and attainable goals.

Back to the guide and maps. There is a lake in southwestern Maine we had often seen and admired from the road. Sebago Lake. If it became too rough for canoeing, and the guide indicated that it often does, we could move over to Long Lake, connected to Sebago by a river and a pond. The State of Maine owns a large tract of land at the northern end of Sebago, with sites for trailers and camping. Our destination was settled.

The evening before departure found the canoe strapped to the car top and the trunk loaded with our supplies. The telephone rang. It was a friend of mine inviting me to play golf the next morning. Sorry, friend, but we're leaving early for a camping and canoeing trip in Maine.

"You intend to sleep in a tent? On the ground? In Maine, in September, when the temperature can go down into the twenties?"

Yes, all that, and we'll canoe each day—weather permitting.

My friend knew of my heart problem, but with typical grace he avoided the subject. But not really, for he asked one more question.

"What are you trying to prove?"

The question startled me. Later it disturbed me. What am I, what are we, two people no longer even middle-aged, trying to prove? Nothing? Something? But why should we, any more than a young couple setting out on a camping trip, be trying to prove something? Why should we even be asked such a question? I had no answers. Morning arrived, and we took off.

Six hours later we drove up to the reception building at the entrance to Sebago Lake State Park. After Labor Day, park services are reduced, and the building was closed. We drove on, passing some of the 287 campsites. Only a few were occupied. The road drew us in a semicircle through the park until we came to the lake. We chose a site with a magnificent view and backed the car into it.

In an hour we were established. We stood back, looked at each other, then at our home for a week. There was a wood picnic table, a stone fireplace, and a refuse can. But the tent that had seemed so large and sturdy in our son's backyard when he had demonstrated it to us now appeared small and frail.

There were several hours of daylight left, so we wrestled the canoe off the car and carried it to the lake. Afloat again. With no destination in mind we drifted along the shore. The silence was pervasive. An hour passed, then two. The sun cast a tapestry of fire on the water. The air that was so warm began to turn chilly. Betty had worn only a light sweater and shorts. To warm ourselves we hastened our paddle strokes and headed for shore.

I found wood and built a fire. It was getting colder by the minute. Decorum called for supper at the picnic table, but we ate it standing before the fire. The sun had gone. I turned from the flames and looked out over the lake. Beauty and life had fled from its face. Like a puppy straying off the leash, my mind went back to our home—the reading lamp over my chair, music on the twin speakers, lights over the dining-room table. The silverware and napkins—*come back here!* And with a slight whimper my mind returned to the campsite. A disembodied voice on the tiny portable radio told us the temperature was now 40 degrees Farenheit.

Betty busied herself washing the few dishes we had used; I dried them. It was dark, and we switched on a battery-operated lamp. The light was pale against the red glow of the dying fire.

The chores were done. No floor to sweep. The pine needles lay undisturbed. No paper to read, no television news. An owl in a nearby tree hooted, and far out on the lake a duck made a quack or two. That was the evening news of the outdoors.

We made small comments about the clarity of the stars seen here and there through the canopy of trees, about the depth of the silence around us, about the cold. Would the sleeping bags keep us warm? Well, we'd pile on all the clothes we could comfortably wear, crawl in, and find out. Each sleeping bag was large enough for one body. No more. Betty couldn't keep me warm, nor I her. We stared at each other. What had we gone and done! We laughed, donned extra sweaters and socks, then struggled into our long, narrow nests.

One might picture Mother Earth's bosom as soft and yielding, comforting and embracing. One might, if one is young. And it might be true, if one could *find* her bosom. Unfortunately, I seemed to have found her spine, and before dawn I had located every vertebra. A lump here, a small, intractable mound there.

Before pitching the tent we had inspected every inch of the ground, searching for small stones, mounds, or depressions that might disturb our slumbers. We caressed the earth with our hands and even uprooted small tufts of witchgrass. No one ever smoothed a sheet more meticulously than we smoothed the soil that was to cradle our bodies. Seismologists know that the deep layers of the earth are in constant motion. Great plates grind and slide and crush and finally slip, causing earthquakes that are sometimes catastrophic. Most of the major active faults are charted and known. But Mother Earth has her little faults, too. One of them is to push up a stone here, a stone there, from under her skin. They emerged from the ground as we lay squirming, thrashing. Sometime during the night we exhausted ourselves, and fell asleep.

There was a sweet smell of pine in the air. I lay on my back and looked at a patch of sunlight on the wall of the tent. Morning. Then I smelled coffee. I struggled out of the sleeping bag and into the bright sunlight. Betty sat at the picnic table, serene and smiling. On the table was an open can of juice. On her plate was a partially consumed pancake.

A hot shower in the nearby building helped ease kinks out of my back, shoulders, and neck. A hot breakfast helped even more. Then we headed for the lake.

So commenced the days of our canoeing, the nights of our camping. During that first full day, the earth must have turned her bosom to us. Or perhaps we were too tired to stay awake. Whatever, our slumbers from then on were those of innocent babes.

The third evening we walked down to the lake's edge. A rising moon laid a luminescence on the water. A breeze caused the pine needles over our heads to whisper among themselves. I trotted back to the car and hauled out the paddles. We'd never ventured onto the water at night, either here or at home. It was keenly exciting.

A hundred yards or so off shore we shipped our paddles and sat. The ripples on the water ceased their slaps at the canoe as we drifted to a stop. No sound now. No motion. The air was cold, but we wore heavy sweaters and slacks. Summer was falling asleep. Before long this lake, too, would drop off into deep slumber under a thick blanket of ice and snow.

I gazed at the moon and tried to believe that human beings had walked across its face. So distant. Another world.

Two people, wife and husband, alone in infinity. I felt the canoe move slightly. Betty had shivered. Was it the cold, or something far deeper? In the distance a loon called, its sound carrying clear and terribly lonely across the water to our yellow canoe. One call, almost hysterical. Then silence. A minute passed. The loon waited, then called again. Somewhere out there where moon rays struck the sharp edges of tiny waves and shattered into a million glittering shards, another loon should reply. But there was none. A third time the loon made its sound, but the call broke into a despairing, clattering cry. The loon, too, was alone on the lake. It called no more.

As though reading each other's thoughts, we turned the canoe. Our home, our tent, sat among the black pines. We needed to get there. Home, to a tent that would hold us warm until another day.

The fifth day we sought and found the mouth of the Songo River, the stream our Appalachian guide told us connected the two lakes, Sebago and Long. The Songo should have been called the Snake. It twists and turns and writhes, with some straightaways scarcely longer than 15 canoe lengths.

There is little if any current in the river, and the canoe glides along almost of its own will. Again, silence. Only the drip of slender threads of water from the paddles. No boats, no other humans. Far away a chain saw coughs, clears its throat, then snarls at a tree. But that is far away.

We come around a bend. Betty's back straightens. Her paddle stays submerged. Even one drop of water might disturb what she sees. A slight motion of her head leads my eyes to the shore where a doe stands with her forefeet on the sandy bottom of the river's edge. We watch motionless. Only the canoe moves. The deer's head jerks up from the water. She stares at us.

The canoe will not stop. It moves to within perhaps 75 feet of the deer. She cannot bear to have us any closer. With a leap she whirls and bolts into the woods.

We relax and talk a bit. A deer, taking a drink of water. We saw it, on the shores of the Songo River.

Riparian woods: maple, oak, alder, evergreen. Like an artist who begins painting his canvas from the top, autumn has begun tinting the woods of the north. A maple tree flames scarlet; an alder is yellow. An oak's leaves have taken the patina and color of cordovan leather. One leaf, the pink of alpenglow, lies prostrate in the water at our side. The first victim to fall.

And white sandy beaches, too. At noon the bow of the canoe gently nudges the shore. We step onto the sand, unwrap sandwiches, take soft drinks from the cooler. Betty has cocooned my three pills in aluminum foil. Three before each meal for as long as I live. That is no hardship.

We loll on the beach. A film of cloud has moved into the sky. It seems to confirm the weather report of the previous evening from Portland: Rain, commencing tomorrow. But this is today.

There is still warmth in the sun. We stretch out on the sand and turn our faces up. After a rest we wade about in the chill river water, then climb back into the canoe and shove on. There are miles yet to Long Lake, then more than four miles back down the river and another mile or more on Sebago to our camp. It's not a challenge. It's not a chore. It's life and living. I remember Bruce Bliven's thoughts on old age. I feel like a young man. And Betty is once more a young and beautiful woman.

The next morning we roll the sleeping bags up and bind them. We remove the tent poles. The tent falls to the ground, signaling the end of an adventure. We fold the tent in on itself, roll and pack it away in the trunk of the car. Where a short time ago the campsite was home, it now reverts to the thing it was designed to be—a place for campers. It is our home no longer.

We walk down to the shore of the lake. Sebago shows us its teeth—two-foot waves with whitecaps race toward us. They dare us to come out today. The sky is dark and low on the water, and a few drops of cold rain ride the wind into our faces. We lift the canoe, our bright yellow canoe, carry it to the car, and hoist it aboard. Now, capsized on its carrier, it, like our campsite, loses value.

Once more we return to the lake. Heavy rain will start soon. But suddenly the sun is bright again, and the lake turns as blue as the sky it mirrors. The Songo River invites us to venture farther, rounding this turn, then the next.

Has there ever been a song without words or music? A song that no voice has sung, no instrument played? A song of peace and tranquillity, when the heart is full and the spirit soars? A celebration of a time when heaven and earth are one, in quiet yet in perfect harmony? If so, it must be the song I hear now.

"What are you trying to prove?" my friend the golfer had asked. Nothing very earth-shaking, I suppose. Only that happiness is indeed worth the chase, whatever your age.

Next time a sunrise steals your breath or a meadow of flowers leaves you speechless, remain that way. Say nothing, and listen as heaven whispers, "Do you like it? I did it just for you."

MAX LUCADO

At last, the soft hues of dawn turn bright with the new day.

WHERE THE SUN ALWAYS RISES

BY
MARNIE O. MAMMINGA

"Get up! Get up!" my mother whispers. My eyes flash open in the predawn gray. Sleepily, I look around the screened-in porch of our family's log cabin, where we spend our summer weeks. I take in the dock-green porch swing, the birch-leg table, the twin bed where my sister sleeps, the smoky glass of the kerosene lantern. My face feels the coolness of the early-morning air.

I relax and curl deeper beneath the blankets' warmth.

"Get up!" my mother whispers again. "The sunrise is glorious!" Careful not to let the screen door slam, she sets off down to the lake.

Get up to see the sunrise? The last thing this fourteen-year-old wants to do is leave a warm bed to see the sun rise. It's freezing out there.

My seventeen-year-old sister pushes back her covers and sits up. I make a supreme effort and struggle out too. We grab my father's World War II army blankets and wrap them tightly around our cotton nighties. Our pace is quick. One of us misses catching the screen door. It slams.

Gingerly, we pick our way over slippery rocks and prickly pine needles, down 49 dew-covered log steps to the shore. We catch our breath and look up. Across the lake, a sliver of brilliant red crests the top of the shadowed forest. It silhouettes our mother on the lake shore, the first light catching the soft red of her hair.

Hues of lavender, rose, and amber begin to pulsate in the sky. High above, in the soft blue, a lone star still sparkles. Silver mist rises gently from the lake. All is still.

Suddenly, the curve of a brilliant sun bursts through the dark forest. The world begins to awaken. A blue heron rises from a distant shore and gently fans its way over the water. Two ducks make a rippled landing near our dock, while a loon skims along the edge of a nearby island, hunting its morning food.

Breathing the chill air, the three of us draw our blankets closer. At last, the soft hues of dawn turn bright with the new day. The star fades. My sister and I take one more look and race back to bed.

My mother is reluctant to leave the sunrise amphitheater. It is a while before I hear her reach the top step and gently close the porch door.

"Get up! Get up!" I whisper to my adolescent sons sleeping in the old metal beds on the cabin porch. "Come see the sunrise! It's awesome!"

I watch as they snatch the World War II army blankets from their beds and stumble out the porch door. It slams. Gingerly, they maneuver over slippery rocks and prickly pine needles down 49 dew-covered log steps to the lake shore.

Their grandmother, her red hair now streaked with white, is already there. She greets us silently with a bright smile, gathers her blanket closer, and turns toward the east.

At last, the soft hues of dawn turn bright with the new day.

My sons watch intently as the rich colors of the sunrise soar into the sky. It isn't long before the lake awakens at the flap of a blue heron's wings and the melodic call of a loon.

"Isn't it beautiful?" I whisper. The boys nod silently. Before long, they grab the tails of their frayed blankets and race back up the steps to the warmth of their beds.

My mother and I stay. Standing close, we watch the swirls of pearl mist rise and the graceful glide of an eagle high overhead. Our faces warm in the early sun.

We turn and begin the slow climb up the old log stairs. Halfway up, I look back to see how my mother is doing. But she's not on the stairs. She has changed her mind. Through the trees I can see her, still on the shore, lingering in the light.

For the mind disturbed, the still beauty of dawn is nature's finest balm.

EDWIN WAY TEALE

THE BOY WHO TALKED WITH DOLPHINS

BY
PAULA MCDONALD

It began as a deep rumble, shattering the predawn silence. Within minutes on that January morning in 1994, the Los Angeles area was in the grip of one of the most destructive earthquakes in its history.

At Six Flags Magic Mountain theme park, 20 miles north of the city, three dolphins were alone with their terror. They swam frantically in circles as heavy concrete pillars collapsed around their pool and roof tiles crashed into the water.

Forty miles to the south, twenty-six-year-old Jeff Siegel was thrown from his bed with a jarring thump. Crawling to the window, Jeff looked out at the convulsing city and thought of the creatures who mattered more to him than anything else in the world. *I've got to get to the dolphins,* he told himself. *They rescued me, and now they need me to rescue them.*

To those who had known Jeff from childhood, a more unlikely hero could not have been imagined.

Jeff Siegel was born hyperactive, partially deaf, and lacking normal coordination. Since he couldn't hear words clearly, he developed a severe speech impediment that made it almost impossible for others to understand him. As a preschooler, the small sandy-haired child was taunted as a "retard" by other kids.

Even home was no refuge. Jeff's mother was unprepared to deal with his problems. Raised in a rigid, authoritarian household, she was overly strict and often angry at his differences. She simply wanted him to fit in. His father, a police officer in their middle-class Los Angeles community of Torrance, worked extra jobs to make ends meet and was often gone 16 hours a day.

Anxious and frightened on the first day of kindergarten, five-year-old Jeff climbed over the schoolyard fence and ran home. Furious, his mother hauled him back to school and forced him to apologize to the teacher. The entire class overheard. As the mispronounced and barely intelligible words were dragged out of him, he became instant prey for his classmates. To fend off the hostile world, Jeff kept to isolated corners of the playground and hid in his room at home, dreaming of a place where he could be accepted.

Then one day when Jeff was nine, he went with his fourth-grade class to Los Angeles's Marineland. At the dolphin show, he was electrified by the energy and exuberant friendliness of the beautiful animals. They seemed to smile directly at him, something that happened rarely in his life. The boy sat transfixed, overwhelmed with emotion and a longing to stay.

By the end of that school year, Jeff's teachers had labeled him emotionally disturbed and learning disabled. But testing at the nearby Switzer Center for children with disabilities showed Jeff to be average-to-bright, though so anxiety-ridden that his math-test score came out borderline retarded. He transferred from the public school to the center. Over the next two years he became less anxious, and his academic achievement improved dramatically.

At the start of seventh grade he returned, unwillingly, to public school. Tests now showed his IQ in the 130s, the gifted range. And years of therapy had improved his speech. But to classmates Jeff was still the same victim.

Seventh grade was unfolding as the worst year of Jeff's life—until the day his father took him to Sea World in San Diego. The minute the boy saw the dolphins, the same rush of joy welled up in him. He stayed rooted to the spot as the sleek mammals glided past.

Jeff worked to earn money for an annual pass to Marineland, closer to his home. On his first solo visit, he sat on the low wall surrounding the dolphin pool. The dolphins, accustomed to being fed by visitors, soon approached the astonished boy.

The first to swim over was Grid Eye, the dominant female in the pool. The 650-pound dolphin glided to where Jeff sat and remained motionless below him. *Will she let me touch her?* he wondered, putting his hand in the water. As he stroked the dolphin's smooth skin, Grid Eye inched closer. It was a moment of sheer ecstasy for the young boy.

The outgoing animals quickly became the friends Jeff had never had, and he began to live from visit to visit. And since the dolphin area was isolated at the far end of Marineland, Jeff often found himself alone with the playful creatures.

One day Sharky, a young female, glided just below the surface until her tail was in Jeff's hand and then stopped. *Now what?* he wondered. Suddenly Sharky dived a foot or so below the surface, pulling Jeff's hand and arm underwater. He laughed and pulled back without letting go. The dolphin dived again, deeper. Jeff pulled back harder. It was like a game of tug-of-war.

When Sharky surfaced to breathe, boy and dolphin faced each other for a minute, Jeff laughing and the dolphin openmouthed and grinning. Then Sharky circled and put her tail back in Jeff's hand to start the game again.

The boy and the 300- to 800-pound animals often played tag, with Jeff and the dolphins racing around the pool to slap a predetermined point, or giving each other hand-to-flipper high-fives. To Jeff, the games were a magical connection that he alone shared with the animals.

Even when there were summer crowds of 500 around the pool, the gregarious creatures recognized their friend and swam to him whenever he wiggled his hand in the water. Jeff's acceptance by the dolphins boosted his confidence, and he gradually emerged from his dark shell. He enrolled in a course at a nearby aquarium and devoured books on marine biology. He became a walking encyclopedia on dolphins and, to his family's amazement, braved his speech impediment to become a volunteer tour guide.

In 1983 Jeff wrote an article for the American Cetacean Society's newsletter, describing his experiences with the Marineland dolphins. He was unprepared for the result: embarrassed by the extent to which he'd been playing with the dolphins without the park's knowledge, Marineland management revoked his pass. Jeff returned home numb with disbelief.

For their part, Jeff's parents were relieved. They could see no benefit to the time their strange, misfit son was spending with dolphins—no benefit until a day in June 1984 when Bonnie Siegel took an unexpected long-distance phone call. That evening she asked her son, "Did you enter some kind of contest?"

Sheepishly Jeff confessed that he'd written an essay for a highly coveted Earthwatch scholarship worth more than $2000. The winner would spend a month in Hawaii with dolphin experts. Now, telling his mother about it, he expected a tirade. Instead she said quietly, "Well, you won."

Jeff was ecstatic. Best of all, it was the first time that his parents realized he might achieve his dream of someday sharing his love of dolphins.

Jeff spent the month in Hawaii, teaching strings of commands to dolphins to test their memories. In the fall, he fulfilled another condition of the scholarship by giving a talk on marine mammals to fellow students at Torrance High School. Jeff's report was so enthusiastic that it earned him, at last, grudging respect from his peers.

The sky is the daily bread of the eyes.

RALPH WALDO EMERSON

After graduation, Jeff struggled to find work at various marine-research jobs, supplementing the low pay with minimum-wage moonlighting. He also obtained an associate's degree in biology.

In February 1992, he showed up in the office of Suzanne Fortier, director of marine-animal training at Six Flags Magic Mountain. Though holding down two jobs, he wanted to do volunteer work with Magic Mountain's dolphins on his days off. Fortier gave him the chance—and was immediately amazed. Of the 200 volunteers she'd trained in ten years, she'd never seen anyone with Jeff's intuitive ability with dolphins.

In one instance, her crew needed to move a sick 600-pound dolphin named Thunder to another park. The animal had to be transported in a nine-by-three-foot tank. During the journey, Jeff insisted on riding in the truck bed with Thunder's tank to try to calm the anxious animal. When Fortier later called from the cab of the truck to ask how Thunder was doing, Jeff replied, "He's fine now. I'm cradling him." *Jeff's actually in the tank with Thunder!* Fortier realized. For four hours, Jeff floated inside the cool tank, holding Thunder in his arms.

Jeff continued to amaze coworkers with his rapport with the animals. His favorite at Magic Mountain was Katie, a 350-pound, eight-year-old dolphin who greeted him exuberantly and swam with him for hours.

Once again, as at Marineland, Jeff could interact with the dolphins and find affection in return. Little did he dream how severely his love would be tested.

As Jeff struggled to reach Magic Mountain on the morning of the earthquake, freeways were collapsing, and caved-in roads often forced him to backtrack. *Nothing is going to stop me,* he vowed.

When Jeff finally reached Magic Mountain, the water in the dolphin pool was halfway down the 12-foot-deep pool, and more was draining steadily from a crack in the side. The three dolphins there when the quake hit—Wally, Teri, and Katie—were in a frenzy. Jeff lowered himself to a ledge five feet down and tried to calm them.

To ease the dolphins through the continuing tremors, Jeff attempted to distract them by playing games, but it didn't work. Worse, he had to reduce their food: the pool's filtration system had shut down, creating the additional risk that an accumulation of their body waste would further contaminate the water.

Jeff remained with the dolphins that night as temperatures fell into the 30s. He was still there through the next day, and the next, and the next. Other staffers trickled in and prepared to move the dolphins.

On the fourth day a road opened, and staffers secured a truck to transfer Wally, Teri, and Katie to the dolphin pool at Knott's Berry Farm. But first, someone had to get them into their transport tanks.

Transporting a dolphin is normally a routine procedure, after it has been safely guided through a tunnel and hoisted on a canvas sling. But the water level in the connecting tunnel was too low for the animals to swim through. The three dolphins would have to be caught in open water and then maneuvered into canvas slings.

Staffer Etienne Francois and Jeff volunteered for the job. As much as he trusted the dolphins, Jeff knew the likelihood of getting hurt or bitten by them in an open-water capture was almost 100 percent.

Wally was easily removed from the pool, but Teri and Katie became erratic. Each time Jeff and Etienne closed in on Katie, the powerful dolphin fended them off with her hard, pointed beak.

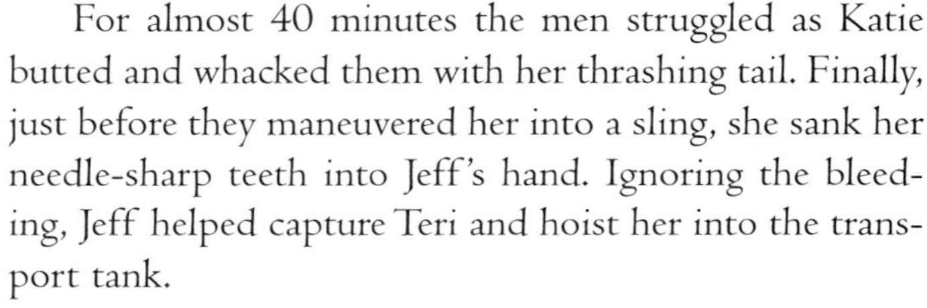

For almost 40 minutes the men struggled as Katie butted and whacked them with her thrashing tail. Finally, just before they maneuvered her into a sling, she sank her needle-sharp teeth into Jeff's hand. Ignoring the bleeding, Jeff helped capture Teri and hoist her into the transport tank.

When the dolphins reached Knott's Berry Farm, Katie was exhausted—but calmer. Later, Fortier told friends that Jeff's courage and leadership had been essential in safely transporting the dolphins.

Today, Jeff is a full-time dolphin trainer at Marine Animal Productions in Gulfport, Mississippi, where he organizes programs for schools.

One day, before he left for Mississippi, Jeff gave a demonstration to 60 children from the Switzer Center at one of the aquariums where he had taught. He saw that a boy named Larry had slipped off to play alone. Realizing Larry was an outcast, as he himself had been, Jeff called him forward and asked the boy to stand next to him. Then Jeff plunged his arms into a nearby tank and hauled out a harmless but impressive three-foot horn shark. As the children gasped, he allowed Larry to carry the dripping creature proudly around the room.

After the session, Jeff received a letter reading: "Thank you for the magnificent job you did with our children. They came back glowing from the experience. Several told me about Larry getting to carry the shark. This was probably the happiest and proudest moment of his life! The fact that you were once a student here added to it. You are a model of hope that they, too, can 'make it' in life." The letter was from Janet Switzer, the center's founder.

For Jeff, that afternoon held an even more gratifying moment. As he spoke, he saw his mother and father in the audience, watching intently. From the look on their faces, Jeff could tell they were proud of their son at last.

Jeff has never earned more than $14,800 a year in his life, yet he considers himself a rich man and an exceptionally lucky one. "I'm completely fulfilled," he says. "The dolphins did so much for me when I was a child. They gave me unconditional love. When I think about what I owe the dolphins . . ." His voice trails off momentarily, and he smiles. "They gave me life. I owe them everything."

THE DUCK AND THE DACHSHUND

BY
PARIS PERMENTER

"Would you like a baby duck?" a friend asked one April day when I was thirteen.

"Sure," I replied, picking up the yellow powder puff and deciding to call her Daisy. I had already been through myriad pets, ranging from abandoned birds to captured ants. What could be better than a duckling?

We lived in an old house in a small Texas town. Our large, fenced yard would keep Daisy safe, but until she grew bigger, my mother suggested that I keep Daisy on an enclosed back porch. There was only one problem—Peanut.

Every neighborhood has at least one dog that slows bicycling children and worries the mailman. Usually the dog is the size of a small pony.

But Peanut was a dachshund—with a long list of dislikes. He didn't like people taller than he was, which ruled out most of the population. He didn't like bicycles or cars. And he had tried to attack so many people (or, rather, their ankles) that he was now confined to our yard.

"If Peanut gets at that duck, there won't even be a pile of feathers left," my mother said. "As soon as Daisy's too big for the porch, we'll take her to your Uncle John's farm."

The spring days grew warmer and Daisy grew larger. By May, she was eager to explore beyond the porch.

Late one afternoon a Texas-size thunderstorm blew in, churning up the sky with a rash of dark clouds. Suddenly a trash-can lid sailed across the yard. I ran out to retrieve it, and Daisy followed me into the yard. I ran after her, but the dachshund got to the duck first.

"Peanut! Stop!" I shouted over the roaring wind.

By the time I reached them—expecting Daisy's feathers to be hanging from Peanut's jaws—the two were quietly staring into each other's eyes. Peanut sniffed at Daisy, who pecked at Peanut's ear.

A loud clap of thunder shook the yard. I tucked Daisy under one of my arms, Peanut burrowed under the other, and I headed back inside the house.

From that day on, there was no separating duck and dachshund. Daisy moved into the backyard with Peanut. When she wasn't floating in his waterbowl, she was napping beside him under a large oak tree.

One hot July morning I went into the yard, but no animals were in sight. "Daisy! Peanut!" I called. A brown head poked out of the doghouse, followed by a white head. Together, the pair waddled toward me. That is, until something caught Peanut's eye. In a flash, he was off and running, barking at a car. Flapping her wings and quacking loudly, Daisy was right behind him. She was learning to be a watchdog.

Things went smoothly for the rest of the summer. Peanut and Daisy were together constantly. Their house bore both their names above the door.

Then one autumn morning, I found Peanut whimpering in the back of the dog-and-duck house. He was paralyzed from the middle of his back down to his tail. Full of anxiety, we took him to the vet.

"Peanut has ruptured a disc in his spine," the vet said. "It's common in dachshunds because of their long backs. I'll operate on him tomorrow, and you can take him home in a few days—if everything goes right. But he'll need to learn to walk again. You'll have to move his legs for him, make him walk. Otherwise, he'll have to be put to sleep."

We left the vet's office in tears, not daring to look back at Peanut. Wordlessly, we drove home, to find Daisy flapping her wings, roaming the yard looking for her friend.

Peanut survived the operation, and a week later we brought him home. Daisy was atop the dog-and-duck house when we drove in. She half-ran, half-flew to the fence. Sadly, we couldn't turn Peanut loose to play. He would have to stay on the porch until his incision healed.

Peanut lay on an old quilt, unable to move anything but his head and front paws. He still had no control over the back half of his body. But at least he was home.

After the first day, we moved Peanut next to the screen door. Daisy sat on the porch steps, quacking and pecking at the screen—as if offering encouragement to her sick friend.

The next week, we took Peanut back for a checkup. "Has he tried to walk yet?" the vet asked, frowning when we said no.

"Peanut must exercise those legs before the muscles deteriorate. If he doesn't begin walking in the next two weeks, he may never walk again."

On the way home we bought a galvanized tub, long enough for Peanut to swim several strokes before turning around. After filling the tub with water, we placed it in the sun to warm up.

An hour later, I carried Peanut to the tub. The moment Daisy saw him she raced across the yard, flapping her wings and quacking. Peanut barked and pathetically tried to wag his paralyzed tail.

Daisy watched as I eased Peanut into the tub. Peanut hated the water and held his head high to keep his long ears from touching it. Only

Daisy seemed eager to get in—so eager that we took her to the porch so he could have the tub to himself.

I held Peanut by his shoulders and pulled him through the water, looking for some sign of movement from his legs. For the next hour, Mother and I moved his legs back and forth to simulate movement, but they remained lifeless.

Mother lifted Peanut out of the tub and onto a towel. "Get Daisy," she said. "We'll let her play in the tub before we pour the water out."

The moment the screen door was opened, Daisy ran to Peanut. She pecked his ears, and he barked with pleasure. Then she plunged in.

Peanut watched her splashing and quacking with delight as she paddled back and forth. Then he stood on his front feet and dragged the back of his body toward the tub.

"I think Peanut wants to get back in the water!" I shouted. Carefully, I lifted him into the tub with Daisy.

Just as Daisy had always tried to copy Peanut, now Peanut was copying her. He paddled with his front legs, pulling his body behind him as I supported him with one hand. He swam several lengths, pushed along by Daisy's urgent quacking. I moved his back legs to simulate movement while he paddled.

For the next hour, the pair swam back and forth, until finally I took Peanut out. Daisy jumped out of the tub and stood beside me as I carefully dried Peanut.

And then it happened. Daisy was pecking his ear when I saw it—Peanut was slowly wagging his tail!

From that day on progress was steady. We continued his daily therapy sessions in the tub (always accompanied by Daisy), and within a week he was swimming on his own, front and back legs in motion. The vet smiled when Peanut walked into his office two weeks later. "I never thought I'd see the day," he confessed.

The summer days soon turned cooler, and fall temperatures caused the pair to be more active than ever, chasing each other playfully through the yard, barking (and quacking) at visitors, or chasing squirrels.

A year passed, and the urgency of Peanut's crisis faded from our memories. We took our pets' special relationship for granted, much as we did our love for one another.

To sit in the shade on a fine day, and look upon verdure is the most perfect refreshment.

JANE AUSTEN

Then one morning we found Daisy lying still in the back of the dog-and-duck house. Peanut was licking her limp neck. It was an uncommon end for an uncommon duck. Daisy had died by choking—on one of Peanut's dog bones.

Whining softly, Peanut followed us as my father tenderly lifted Daisy from their house and buried her under the large oak tree. Twice, Peanut tried to dig up the grave.

Life went on without Daisy, but Peanut seemed to lack enthusiasm. He didn't bother barking at visitors or chasing squirrels. He spent much more time napping in the winter sun.

By the following May, he seemed to have aged many years. With sadness, but perhaps no surprise, we found him one morning, curled up in the dark recesses of the doghouse. Like an echo from the past, his back was paralyzed once again.

Peanut had another operation, and after a week of recuperation, we carried him out to the tub where we had all spent so many hours with Daisy. Peanut refused to cooperate.

"Please, Peanut. Try to swim," I encouraged him, trying to push back the tears.

Day after day, we carried him to the tub, gently lowering him into the water, massaging his legs. For two weeks, we tried to coax him into swimming as he had done before.

But soon we had to accept the reality that Peanut would not move again. Without Daisy to encourage him, he remained an invalid, refusing finally even food and drink.

Three weeks after the operation, Peanut made one last trip to the veterinarian's office, where we tearfully said good-bye to him. Even the vet's eyes glistened when he carried Peanut away.

It has been many years since Peanut and Daisy were part of my life. But I still like to think that somewhere the dog and the duck are together—barking and quacking and having a fine old time.

MY MIDNIGHT SWING

BY
MICHAEL WELZENBACH

From the perch of my apartment's high balcony I had noticed them—these young aspiring pilots, high-jumpers, and daredevils. I'd envied their grace and enthusiasm as they soared high over the heads of their companions. I often wished I, too, could hurtle through the air with such dizzying delight.

Summer progressed, the evenings balmy and electric with the promise of fun. And the temptation was great. Yet every time I felt the urge to race to the playground, I reasoned the impulse away. *What on earth are you thinking?* I reprimanded myself. *A grown man down there on the swings? What would everyone think?*

No, the idea was ridiculous. I had bills to pay, chores to attend to. Leisure time should be spent in adult pursuits—a hike in the country or a trip to the mall.

I stopped watching them. I put a low chair on the balcony, so all I could see were the roofs of other apartment buildings and the fitful late-summer sky.

But I could still hear those giggling voices floating up from below. And then late one Saturday night after a grueling week, as I sat feeling positively ancient, there came to me again, like a faint echo, the sound of children playing.

I flicked off the lights in the living room and opened the sliding doors to the balcony. But for the yellow pools cast by the parking lot lamps, all was dark and peaceful.

Stepping out into the moist night air, I looked down to the playground. There was no one there. *Well, of course not,* I chided myself. *It's nearly midnight. You're hearing things. What you need is a good night's sleep.*

Yet something told me differently, and this time I didn't reason it away. With sudden determination, I went inside, pulled on a sweater, and walked out the door.

The dew-moistened grass tickled my sandaled feet on the way to the playground. Here and there above me a window glowed with the flickering light of a television. I was completely alone.

The monkey bars loomed against the starry sky. A tall slide described a shiny, graceful S to the ground. The seesaws sat at angles.

And there, dangling silently on their chains, hung three swings. For a long moment I looked at them, feeling suddenly timid and as though dozens of neighbors were watching from their windows. But it was too late to turn back, and the swings beckoned as strongly as they had when I was a boy.

I walked to the middle swing and sat in its wide rubber sling. Grabbing the chains, I gave a sharp pull. Yes, they'd hold me all right.

With a mighty heave I kicked up and backward with my feet. In an instant I was rocketing forward, my toes pointed to the stars.

It was exhilarating. Even wistful imagination hadn't prepared me for the sheer, tummy-turning thrill of dangling for a long second at the end

of the sweeping arc and the sudden plummet backward. I had forgotten how streamlined I felt; how the cool rush of air made my eyes water.

Then I remembered the playground of my youth. In the long summer evenings, when I was six or seven, my brothers and I would race down the hill to the swings. We would dare each other to jump off at the highest point. In those distant days, there seemed nothing on earth that dreaming couldn't make so.

Later there were the swings in the park behind my school. It was a gathering place for young teenagers, where boys met and chatted, sitting idly on the swings. At the appearance of a group of girls, all conversation hushed and any actual swinging stopped. We were glad to see the girls, but terrified nevertheless.

Now, as I pumped the air with my feet and pulled on the chains to propel myself higher, it was hard to believe I had let this much simple fun slip away.

As a boy, I had dreamed of traveling the world, and I had done that. I had dreamed of playing the guitar and the violin, and had struggled along at both with some success. I had dreamed of finding a fossil worthy of a museum, and after 20 years of searching I had done that too.

Mostly, of course, I had dreamed of being a grownup and of doing what I wanted, when I wanted. But as I grew older, I became free like every other adult—free to make decisions, free to clutter my life with all sorts of possessions. But how free had I really become?

Not very, it seemed. For wasn't freedom the self-confidence to stop on impulse and do a somersault on the lawn? To make a snow angel and not be concerned what anyone might think?

Lulled by the rhythmic creaking of the chains on the nighttime swing, I found myself growing unaccountably happy. So my taxes were due. So the car inspection sticker had nearly expired. So that badly needed check hadn't yet turned up in the mailbox. So what? My toes were touching stars and my heart was chuckling.

The next morning when I left my apartment, I ran into my computer-specialist neighbor in the parking lot. "Was that you I saw on the swing last night?" he asked, smirking.

"Indeed it was," I said. "And maybe again tonight."

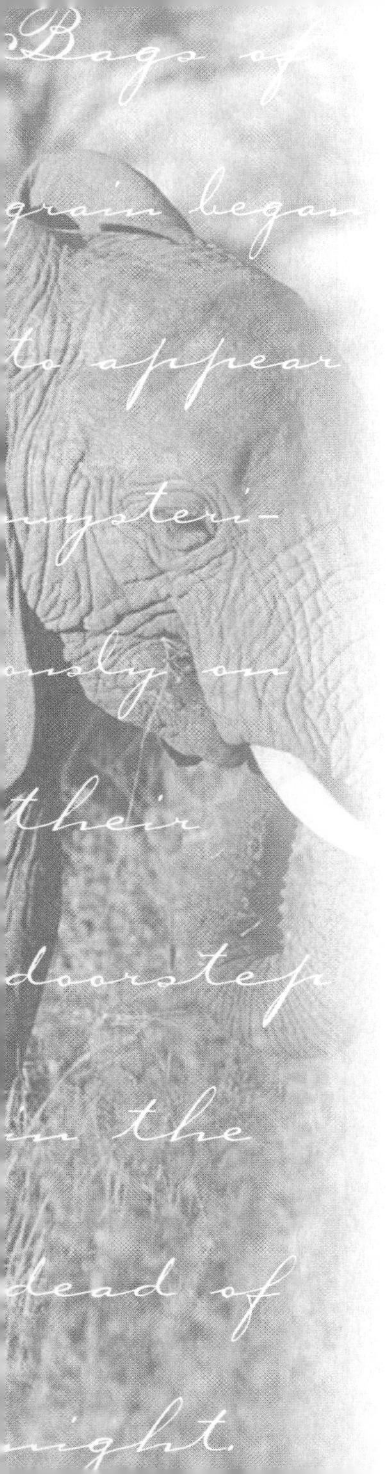

ALL GOD'S CREATURES

BY
NATHAN M. ADAMS

On August 2, 1990, Kuwait's zoo, one of the best-stocked in the Arab world, was ominously quiet. The big cats had not left their dens since dawn. Even the macaws and macaques were silent. Only wolves paced back and forth, pausing to prick their ears at the rumble of artillery and the faint clatter of approaching helicopters. By nightfall, invading Iraqi forces controlled the city.

Thus began a seven-month ordeal of almost indescribable brutality for the zoo's 735 creatures. This is the untold story of two heroic brothers who risked everything to save the most helpless of Saddam Hussein's victims.

Kuwait ceased to exist on August 3, 1990. It would become the nineteenth province of Iraq.

Within hours of the invasion, teams of *mukhabarat*—Iraq's dreaded secret police—were combing neighborhoods for Kuwaiti officials and suspected loyalists. Entire families vanished overnight. Husbands and wives, sons and daughters, were abducted, tortured, and killed.

Like Kuwait's 2.2 million other residents Suleiman Mubarak al-Hoti, a thirty-one-year-old motorcycle policeman, survived one day at a time. He kept his wife and two daughters hidden from marauding Iraqis, and not until the third week of occupation did he even think much about the zoo.

The Kuwait Zoological Gardens had been part of Suleiman's life since he gripped his father's hand and first saw the great bears, sleek panthers, and antic baboons. He knew all the animals by name: Sultan, the tiger from faraway Sumatra; Twiga, the giraffe from the vast African veldt; Tupo, the puma from North America.

Each Friday, after prayers at the mosque, Suleiman would gather his family and make the 20-minute drive to the zoo. While his daughters fed the ducks, he would seek counsel with the larger animals. His favorite was the Indian elephant he called Aziza.

When the elephant spotted the man with a clipped beard, she extended her trunk through the bars in greeting. Suleiman kept cashews and pistachios hidden in his robe. It was their secret game. Aziza found them easily, then rested her trunk on his shoulder and swayed contentedly.

Now Suleiman wondered who was caring for her and the other creatures. Were they being fed and watered regularly? He had to find out for himself. But how? Visitors were no longer permitted there.

Every section of the city had Iraqi roadblocks manned 24 hours a day. Without official papers, he could be arrested as a member of the resistance. Still, Suleiman believed that if he somehow avoided the checkpoints, soldiers guarding the zoo would see he was just an animal lover.

"That's not a wise idea," warned his older brother Ali, a city employee. "Suppose they take you for a spy?" Ali drew a finger across his throat to illustrate the consequences.

Ali, thirty-five, insisted on going too. "But we should have a plan. Perhaps we can find another pair of those red overalls the fire department gave me."

Suleiman nodded. The overalls were surplus, and a friend had given a pair to Ali several months before. But why did he want another?

Ali explained: because the Iraqis respected uniforms, guards might assume the visit was approved and let them enter the zoo. "This will be our way of fighting back," he said.

Suleiman's wife begged him to reconsider. Did the animals mean more to him than his own family? "We are all God's creatures," he replied.

On August 31, the twenty-ninth day of the occupation, Suleiman and Ali put on their firemen's overalls and drove toward the zoo. They had not gone a mile when they were ordered to pull over. Soldiers menaced them with automatic rifles. What were the brothers doing in a security zone?

Ali recited their alibi—an inspection of the zoo for fire and health hazards. "That's odd," one Iraqi said. "I thought that all the animals were dead."

Ali could feel his brother stiffen beside him. Then the guard stepped back and waved them on.

They could smell death a full block away from the zoo gates. A rotting baboon carcass lay in the parking lot; a headless gazelle shriveled in the heat nearby. Suleiman dreaded what they would find inside.

The brothers were taken at gunpoint to the unit's leader. Dead animals were everywhere: the remains of a zebra, a black panther decaying beneath a mound of lime. Iraqis squatted around cook fires, roasting peacocks and ducks that Suleiman's daughters had once fed.

The detachment's commander listened to Ali's story. "Why does the fire department bother?" he asked. "We're going to kill them all sooner or later." However, since the visit was official, he would permit the inspection. They'd be accompanied at all times by an armed escort.

The al-Hotis made their rounds, pantomiming tests of all the firefighting equipment they could locate. The zoo was a wasteland. Air conditioners vital to the survival of northern animals were ripped from windows. Drinking tanks had become a putrid jelly of algae and manure. From the darkness of dens, frightened eyes peered forth.

The brothers tried to take stock. The crocodiles were dead, shot in their pool. A kangaroo was huddled near a palm tree, riddled by gunfire. Cage doors were ajar, and famished monkeys foraged greedily among the heaps of refuse.

Only Aziza, the Indian elephant, seemed unaffected. She stood quietly as they approached, then plodded forward in recognition. When Suleiman let himself through the bars, the elephant lifted her trunk and searched his pockets.

"I'm sorry, old friend," he said, stroking her rough hide. "Nothing today. Maybe tomorrow."

Seeing that there was no hay in her stall and the watering trough was nearly dry, Suleiman approached a soldier and asked who was feeding the animals. A keeper came some mornings, the Iraqi replied. The rest of the staff had fled.

Ali led his brother back to the car. He was already mapping a strategy: the "fire department" had changed its orders. Until further notice, they were permanently assigned to the zoo. With any luck, the Iraqis would not question the change.

By mid-September they had settled into a routine. The Iraqis soon became bored watching them do their chores. First, the brothers cleaned cages and skimmed bathing pools of weeds and scum. Then, they delivered fresh water by hand—an exhausting two-man bucket brigade.

Food was the most urgent need. Suleiman remembered reading that an elephant like Aziza consumes up to 200 pounds of hay a day. A lion could eat a cow in two days. Such amounts would be impossible to supply. Once again, Ali hit on a solution. He knew the location of the city's garbage-collection stations and realized that such waste, though unfit for humans, still contained nourishment. It could spell the difference between survival and death for many animals.

Every day, the brothers crawled through reeking dumpsters hot as ovens, gathering scraps. Gristle, bones, and spoiled meat were set aside for the carnivores; fruit rinds and soggy vegetables were fed to the monkeys, water buffalo, and hippos.

Word spread of their private war to rescue the animals. Bags of grain began to appear mysteriously on their doorstep in the dead of night. It seemed as though the zoo had become a symbol of resistance against the occupiers.

Animals are such agreeable friends—they ask no questions, they pass no criticism.

GEORGE ELIOT

As winter approached, many animals were no more than living skeletons, despite all the brothers' efforts. Ali al-Hoti began to have doubts. Were they simply prolonging the suffering, delaying the inevitable?

The Iraqi occupation authorities announced that all vehicles in Kuwait were to be reregistered. Any car not displaying Iraqi plates would be confiscated and its driver arrested. Ali refused to comply. But he had made a promise; there had to be another means of reaching the zoo.

The answer lay no further away than their own backyard—the family bicycle. With Suleiman perched on the handlebars, the brothers wobbled onto the highway every day at noon. It was an eight-mile pedal to the garbage dumps. The added weight of full trash bags made the journey to the zoo agonizing.

So far, the brothers' presence at the zoo had been tolerated. In October, however, the al-Hotis were searched by guards they did not recognize and told to reapply for permission to enter.

Ali sensed danger. The new troops were an undisciplined rabble. They had already killed an antelope, and an injured Syrian bear was moaning softly in a corner of a cage.

The brothers were brought before an officer with piggish eyes. "I am Abu," he announced. "I'm now in charge." Rising from behind the desk, he placed the muzzle of his pistol against Ali's cheek. "If the animals need so much food, maybe I should let them eat you."

Ali felt his skin crawl. He knew such atrocities were common. Less than a mile from the zoo, Saddam's *mukhabarat* had converted an agricultural building into a human slaughterhouse where tortured shrieks and the volleys of firing squads rang out day and night.

Ali stared straight ahead. He heard the pistol's hammer click back, then snap on an empty chamber. The grinning officer set the gun on the desk. Perhaps an "arrangement" could be worked out, he told them, in return for certain goods and services. Among the items he required were videotape recorders, cassette players, transistor radios, and stereo equipment. Cigarettes and cameras were also acceptable bribes. And there was one thing more: "You will bring me magazines with pictures of naked ladies," he ordered. "Otherwise, you go to the lions. Understand?"

"As you wish," Ali answered, trying to disguise his dismay. The al-Hotis were strict Moslems, for whom possession of pornography was an unthinkable offense. Still, the brothers were the animals' only hope. Somehow, the bribes would have to be met.

They turned to friends and neighbors. A friend donated a VCR, a family next door a cassette player; a smoker promised cigarettes. The Iraqi was pleased. But he had not forgotten the magazines. "The lions are waiting!" he threatened.

For the next few days, guards cursed and beat Ali and Suleiman for the most minor infractions. But after a week, the harassment abruptly ended. The brothers guessed that their tormentor had found his lurid photographs elsewhere. The animals, however, were not as fortunate.

Steadily, the toll rose. The al-Hotis now feared that 75 percent of the animals had died, and most of the others were sick, wounded, or missing. Even Aziza was beginning to fail. Suleiman sometimes found her leaning against the cage as if to conserve strength. To supplement her diet, he shinnied up trees and tore off leafy branches and strips of bark—anything that might be edible.

Ali gave the remaining animals six weeks at most. Only the arrival of the Allies could save them. But news reports were discouraging. Saddam had ignored every deadline to withdraw his forces.

Then in the early morning hours of January 17, 1991, American-led bombers struck deep into Iraq. The attacks continued into February, gradually moving south and isolating Iraqi armored units in Kuwait. Allied soldiers, poised less than 90 miles away in Saudi Arabia, seemed so near—yet so far.

Before leaving the zoo one night, the brothers counted only 42 animals still alive. Many had been shot and eaten by the Iraqis, whose rations were now cut off by the intense bombing. The date was February 23, the two hundred and fifth day of the occupation. It would be the last.

Through the next day, sounds of battle drew closer. The al-Hotis, like most Kuwaitis, stayed indoors and prayed. By evening, U.S. Marine and British armored columns neared the suburbs. Most of Saddam's troops fled. On February 26, Kuwait City was liberated.

When Suleiman and Ali went to the zoo, they were stunned by the carnage. Before abandoning their positions, the Iraqis had turned their weapons on the animals out of spite. *What kind of men would do such things?* Suleiman wondered. *The animals are innocent. They harm no one.*

At the far end of the zoo, Aziza lay motionless in her cage, a deep wound in her shoulder. Suleiman was sure she was dead. He raised the lock and entered her enclosure. When the elephant struggled to her feet, Suleiman saw a tear well in one eye and slowly trickle down her rough cheek.

Suleiman looked at his brother, whose face was twisted in anguish. Ali felt he was about to break. He had just completed a final tally of the animals. There were only 32.

Major Tom Ogilvie-Graham, a veterinarian attached to the crack British Seventh Armored Brigade, rushed to the zoo as soon as he heard rumors of what had happened there. What he found sickened him. The charred remains of a lioness lay in one cage; she had apparently been shot and then set afire. The refrigerator used to store food was an ooze of rotten meat and severed heads—trophies the Iraqis had overlooked in their haste to flee.

Nearing the end of the cage rows, he was amazed to see two figures dressed in bright red. Shouting with joy, Ali and Suleiman ran to greet the major and his squad. Then, in halting English, they described the half-year ordeal.

Ogilvie-Graham could scarcely believe his ears. Without the brothers, it was clear, not a single animal would be alive. The Syrian bear and the elephant concerned him most. Untreated, they could die in a matter of days. Assisted by the two brothers, he searched the zoo for medicines.

Miraculously, they found antibiotics and vitamins buried beneath broken glass and overturned tables in the pharmacy. The major immediately administered them to Aziza and the bear. Then he arranged for a tanker truck to deliver fresh water from the brigade's own reserves.

It was a beginning. At least the remaining animals would last the night; how much longer, he could not say. But help was on the way. By the end of the week, John Walsh, a Boston-based official of the World Society for the Protection of Animals, arrived at the zoo to take charge of the rescue effort.

Within hours, Walsh met with the U.S. Army's three hundred fifty-second Civil Affairs Command, which was coordinating restoration of Kuwait's vital services. He pleaded the animals' case and its urgency. Then he arranged for feed to be trucked in from Saudi Arabia. Overnight, the zoo became a hive of activity.

Allied troops worked with Kuwaiti citizens to remove the mountains of trash and decaying carcasses. Walsh was struck by the irony; here, in the midst of war's savagery, men of different nationalities were pitching in to save the remaining animals in a zoo most never knew existed, in a nation many could not have found on a map six months before.

With huge water tankers arriving twice daily and a regular supply of feed assured, Ogilvie-Graham told Walsh that he felt they were over the worst. Gradually, the animals were gaining weight, and a healthy sheen was returning to the cats' coats. Many might now survive surgery to locate and remove bullets.

The major started with Aziza. Because of the elephant's size, he decided to pinpoint the embedded shrapnel with a mine detector—a technique he'd used to treat several of Queen Elizabeth II's horses cruelly maimed in a 1982 bombing in London. As the al-Hotis watched anxiously, he swept the long-handled instrument over the wound. When electronic signals revealed that the slug had lodged against her shoulder blade, just missing vital organs, the major decided an operation would be riskier than leaving the bullet in place. Aziza seemed to be in no pain, and antibiotics had helped prevent infection. Over time, a cyst would form a protective covering. Assured that there would be no need for surgery and that Aziza would fully recover, the al-Hotis wept with relief.

But some wounds would never heal. A macaque shot by an Iraqi general refused to let anyone near it. The wolves hid in their burrows and fed only at night. When a TV news crew got too close to Aziza's cage, she seized their video camera and crushed it underfoot.

On April 4, Ogilvie-Graham received orders to rejoin his Household Cavalry regiment on duty at Buckingham Palace. He bid a quiet farewell to the al-Hotis, then to the animals he had done so much to save. It was the most satisfying mission he'd ever had, but he regretted leaving, for the rescue of the Kuwait zoo was far from over. His place was taken by Edwin Zemo, a U.S. Army Reserve colonel who ran a small veterinary practice in Baltimore during peacetime. Zemo was dumbfounded to learn that many animals, including two rare Himalayan bears, a gazelle, and a pair of llamas, were returned to the zoo by Kuwaitis who had safeguarded them from Iraqi soldiers during the occupation.

At the end of April, the Syrian bear, which had seemed to be recovering, was discovered dead in its cage. But this was the final casualty. When Zemo and Walsh turned the zoo over to its Kuwaiti administrators at the beginning of May, healing of the animals was largely complete.

Even after Allied troops left, the al-Hotis continued to go to the zoo to help care for the animals. On August 10, while his brother fed the lions, Suleiman visited Aziza. Once more, her trunk searched his robe for treats. She had not forgotten their game.

Suleiman looked over at Ali and their eyes met in an unspoken message. They were home again among friends, among family—among God's creatures.

THE DAMFOOL PLACE

BY
GEORGE P. MORRILL

Years ago, I did an impulsive thing. Deep in the Vermont woods I hacked out a one-acre clearing.

There was no road in to it. I had to carry an axe through a swamp and down a ledge to reach the tree-choked mountainside. Nor was there an immediate purpose for my action. Stove wood grew closer to our cabin, and in our neck of the wild, where self-seeding trees keep you battling for space to breathe, a sensible man clears his home lot first.

Nevertheless, one mulberry twilight in October I started whacking ivory-colored chunks from a tall, gnarled hemlock. The tree tilted against a big maple, but would not fall. I chopped the maple. *It* came to rest against a rugged young oak. By this time, lilac shadows had thickened. I had to leave the trees leaning—a dangerous thing.

When I warned my wife, Phyllis, she lifted an eyebrow at our seven-year-old, Pete. "Watch out," she said. "The Mad Axman is booby-trapping our property."

The next night, I rushed home from work, cleared the brush around the bowed oak, and swung my axe against its straining bark. CRACK! The green roof fell. Sitting in fragrant ferns, I saw a hole to the sky, threaded with dancing sparrows. Ah, breathing space!

In the next five weeks, I knocked down three trees each evening. It became an obsession. Often I chopped in cinder-soft darkness, my blade flashing like a mirror. On weekends, I trimmed the fallen timber and hauled branches to the swamp.

Slowly, the clearing widened. Friends looked in—and shrugged. Only my old farmer-neighbor, Richard Bradley, seemed to understand. "Keep chopping," he said with a chuckle. "The reason will come out when it has a mind to."

By midwinter I had a battlefield. Crisscrossed logs festooned with ice jutted from sudsy drifts. Slugging with the axe, blowing ice lace on my mackinaw collar, I felt muscles harden along my shoulders. Sometimes I shouted for glory.

One cold Saturday, when the sky was slabbed with porcelain clouds, my axe skidded off a limb and hit my left leg. It was a glancing blow, missing the shinbone and not hurting too much. But blood trickled down my boot, red against the snow.

I was about to limp back to the cabin when the thought struck me: *What would a Vermont pioneer have done in this situation?*

I stood still, drinking in the harsh beauty of black-and-white hills. Then I pulled my wool sock over the wound and went back to work.

You see, I *sensed* those long-vanished Vermonters in the shadows all around me. Watching. Judging. Like me, they had struggled to build homesteads on little capital. They, too, had shaped their property with an axe. How they'd snort if I chickened out because of a shin scratch! ("I trust you're not going nuts," said Phyllis later, bandaging my leg.)

Thereafter I was never alone in my project. Invisible settlers looked on, assessing a tree's line of fall, its clean or gnawed-off cut. Once a voice cracked, "Axe a mite dull?" (I swear I heard it—or could it have

been dead branches knocking in the gale?) That night I sharpened the blade with a hand file.

February passed. March. I welcomed knee-deep slush and thundering brooks, skunk cabbage and early robins. My clearing emerged, tawny-wet, from its polar mantle.

A village farmer inspected it. "Why," he said, "you can't get any equipment to the damfool place."

"Exactly," I said, somehow pleased at the idea. The same day I felled *four* trees—under the thoughtful gaze of my spirit friends.

By mid-spring I knew what these ghostly mentors looked like. They were a trio: a red-faced shorty with thick arms, a beanpole with sinewy arms and no teeth, and a wide-shouldered Hercules who slouched against a tree, chewing something. All wore Colonial muslin shirts and had lined, muscular faces. Contemptuous of my lack of plan, they began to put ideas into my head.

Now them trees are down, why not cut a road to pull 'em out?

I hacked a wagonway through the swamp.

Render them logs fireplace-size.

I sawed the timber and stacked it in gigantic heaps.

You need a team and dray for hauling.

I got a logger to bring horses and rubber-tired wagon. The whole family threw wood aboard. We hauled out enough firewood to last seven years.

Now what? We stared at the snag-toothed clearing. "Let's level it for a hayfield," I said. "Bulldozer costs only eight bucks an hour."

It meant going without a long-wanted rug and a valve job for the jeep. But, within the week, a 'dozer snarled through the woods, gouging a road. It uprooted stumps, chewed down the high side of the clearing, and pushed a huge hummock of fill to the low side. After two days, the clearing lay bare, scented with raw topsoil. Beautiful.

Shorty, Beanpole, and Hercules weren't carried away, however. *If you don't seed this muck patch directly, it will go to gullies.*

Okay, okay . . . A neighbor agreed to harrow, sow, and fertilize it for $200. I raised $50 by selling a concrete-block maker, and pledged to pay the rest monthly.

"Just where are we heading?" asked Phyllis cautiously.

I hardly knew. But this clearing had to be!

May slipped in, gauzed with green. Then silver whips of rain lashed the ground. At storm's end, wrinkled gullies had grown to a dozen small canyons.

Plug them run-offs.

Drenched and cursing, I piled stones in the muddy slots. By the time a drying wind appeared, the land was a washboard.

After a week, Phyllis and I returned—in brilliant sunshine—to a delightful shock. The clearing had exploded in wildflowers: pink geranium; snowy clintonia; yellow lady's slippers. New grass tinted the rills, emerald and soft. "Someday we'll fence it in," I whispered reverently.

Someday . . . But not right away. In fact, two decades have passed now. In all that time, season by season, the clearing has demanded our efforts: ditchdigging, tree pruning, mowing by scythe. "It's just a slave lot," my grown sons (four now) complain. "An exercise in nonproduction."

Nonproduction? Why, I've reaped a treasure from this damfool hole in the forest that can't be calculated in money or time.

I've worked out gallons of sweat, listening to the whisper of my blade, inhaling the perfume of warm hay. I've paused to chew grass and absorb the sky. (There has been no next-door busybody to scoff, "That guy's the worst worker I've ever seen—rests every two minutes.") I've sung, recited poetry, even cawed back at a crow who derided my music from a dead elm. I've examined veins of lightning in a bloated June cloud.

Shoveling, muttering to myself, I've stopped wars, climbed Everest, puzzled over God. I've even been healed by the place. Once, when a dear friend was killed in an accident, I trudged in misery over the bumpy turf. Crickets sang. The sun moved on. Nature's sermon returned: *Everything is faithful to its cycle.* I came home restored.

Again, when Pete served his Army hitch in ill-omened Vietnam, I couldn't wait to reach the clearing and lose myself in amnesiac toil.

So, the reason for it all has come clear—as Richard Bradley predicted it would. I carved out that clearing because a man needs a refuge in nature. His chemistry demands a private haunt where he can grapple with cold and heat, life wounds and soul weariness; a place to untether his most secret thoughts. In short, a place to be free.

Today the clearing looks as ragged as usual. I expect a fine crop of black-eyed susans and weeds this summer. Some saffron afternoon, I'll amble over, armed with tools, select a soft place, and stretch out. Dreams and memories will drift in from the forest, along with those familiar phantoms. Shorty, Beanpole, and Hercules will nod their tri-cornered hats and spit.

Got a middling-fair piece of dirt here. Gonna set on it eternal? It'll go to hell if you don't cut them hemlock seedlings.

I'll arise leisurely and take a grip on my scythe . . .

Flowers always make people better; happier and more helpful; they are sunshine, food and medicine to the soul.

LUTHER BURBANK

At such times, one is not man, not spirit, but some-thing in between

COME WALK AT NIGHT!

BY
PETER STEINHART

At midnight, under the brightest moon of summer, I went to the circus. The vast tent was dark. The band instruments had been put away, the tiger cages were covered with tarps, and the clowns and acrobats were asleep. It was as still as a cloud, and very little like a circus. But that did not matter. I had come to see the elephants.

I had seen them during the day, shifting anxiously from foot to foot, shaking their heads as if to dislodge unhappy thoughts. They had seemed driven mad by the noise of the crowd. Now, in the dark, they were very different. Seven lay sprawled on the ground, like shadowy boulders given over to the trust of dreams. Three elephants stood swaying over them, their trunks making gentle tracings on the sides of their sleeping comrades. After the confusion of the day, the elephants seemed at peace with the night, illuminated with a quiet wisdom. And *that* was what I longed to share with them.

In such nighttime moments, I become an explorer. "I have been one acquainted with the night," wrote Robert Frost. "I have walked out in rain and back in rain . . . I have outwalked the furthest city light." The night is one of man's last remaining adventures. If job and family keep me from exploring distant mountains and deserts, there are still the unmapped regions of the night to wander.

Night's gifts are out of the ordinary, *ec-static,* and always unexpected. On a warm summer evening, I have turned to see a full moon, huge and orange as a pumpkin, grinning over a nearby ridge, bursting with mirth and spilling its dazzling light over the hillside. It made me laugh out loud, thrilled me with an exuberance of discovery I had thought only a child could feel. I have stood in mountain meadows with coyotes singing all around me, until the howling and yipping of a dozen wild voices made me feel like a coyote in spirit.

I have been a night walker since I was a boy. The risks of darkness, instead of frightening me, challenged my imagination even then. Tradition holds that night is another country, edged with danger, a metaphor for evil, death, or ignorance. Night is where the devil waits, witches cackle, and faceless animals scurry and hide. But to a boy these adventures are one with Halloween and Never-Never-Land!

Once, for an hour, I stood with a friend in Yosemite National Park, beneath an apple tree and a sliver of September moon, while above us a bear moaned and chuffed and rattled branches, angry at our intrusion but too timid to come down. We knew the bear was afraid of us, but his eerie sounds raised the hair on our necks nevertheless.

Resuming night walks as an adult, I found that grown-up anxieties had given new edge to the adventure. The flapping wings of a mourning dove were enough to chill my bones. So, on my first night walks into the hills near my California home, I carried a flashlight and a stick, timorously arming myself against the unknown.

But gradually I dispensed with my bubble of light, and climbed higher; one night, looking down on the dazzle of San Francisco, far below, I began to see how sad is all that energy burning in the night—so intense the astronomers in the hills complain they cannot see the stars.

The sadness of city light, the hard, staring glow of neon, made the night less fearful to me. Outdoors, in the dark, one gradually outgrows the sense of risk, and then the night becomes something kinder and more generous, a meeting ground of reason and emotion, a place where mind and soul can work together.

By day, we put away our feelings, and are wonders of reason. But we feel we must be more. We have complex and powerful emotions. Reason and feeling ought to go together. I suspect that their natural meeting place is in the dark.

But night is a puzzle that reason cannot adequately answer, or emotion entirely rule. The ancients linked night with poetry, magic, and madness; we know only that there is something in us daylight leaches out. The dark need not make one fearful; it can make one reverent. At night we are closer to our spirit natures. So night walking is a quest for spirit. And I believe that I have caught fleeting glimpses of the quarry.

Summer nights are a good time to hunt. Near my home, the moon bathes the dry brown grass in almost enough light to read by. Walking the hills at night, one must trust as much to nose and ears as to eyes, which ties you to the creatures of the night. An owl flashes across the sky, as bright as quicksilver, and you can feel the concentration in his eye, taste his longing for mouse. A sleeping dove bolts from a bush, terrified by the nightmare of your approach, and your heart flies off with the bird. At such times, one is not man, not spirit, but something in between: a movement, a thought, a feeling. It is at once comforting and exhilarating.

To those who haven't tried it, I say, *come walk at night.* Begin in your own backyard. Go from there to safe rural roads, ideal in moonlight. Take your bubble of light and protective walking stick along at first, if you must; you'll soon discard them. For all that is required to seek night's adventures and gifts is an open heart and a desire to understand. At night, wrote Henry Beston, "a new door opens for the human spirit."

That is why I have come to see the circus elephants tonight. One of them turns toward me. It seems like an invitation, so I step closer to her. Without opening an eye, she slowly snakes her trunk in my direction. Noiselessly, she sniffs. Then she slides her trunk gently across my face. Her gesture makes me feel as if I were really one of them. As I stand beside her, befriended, I am sharing the ponderous dreams of giants, sharing the peace of the night.

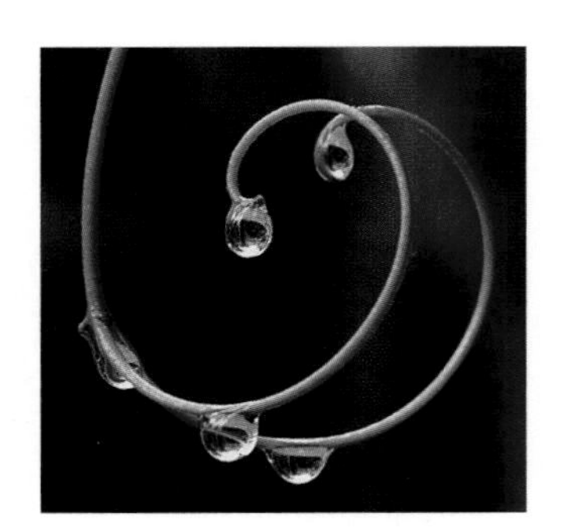

One of summer's best fragrances is neither fruit nor flower; it is the smell of rain when the first drops come down and sink into the grateful hot earth or onto hot, dry stones. If peace has a fragrance, it is the fragrance of this rain.

RACHEL PEDEN

ANDY GOOSE STEPS OUT

BY
JO COUDERT

"You've got a sick goose over there," Gene Fleming remarked to his sister-in-law as they walked to his car. He had stopped by Billee Schuck's farm in Harvard, Nebraska, to pick up some ducklings for his pond, and he noticed a goose that kept toppling over.

Billee didn't even look around. "Naw, that's Andy," she said. "He was born without feet."

With the ducklings safely stowed, Fleming went over to look at the handicapped goose. "You're a gutsy fella," he said as Andy, flapping wildly, tried to run away. The gray goose looked like a little boy on his first pair of stilts. His legs, thin as twigs, ended in calloused knobs the size of silver dollars. The only way Andy could stay upright was to run as fast as he could until he pitched forward on his breast. He fell now, and Gene reached out to smooth his feathers. Because geese tend to be peevish, he expected to get nipped; but Andy was quiet under his touch.

Gene kept thinking about the crippled goose as he headed home to his 91-acre spread in Hastings. He felt an appeal in those shoe-button eyes as Andy lay forlornly on the ground, his breast caked with mud.

Gene though about his Shriner's dedication to helping crippled children. *That goose is just as helpless as a little child,* he told himself. *I ought to be able to do something for him.*

Gene put his inventive mind to work, just as he had years before when he saw cows tormented by insect bites. That time, he designed a scratching device that cows could rub against to release a dose of insecticide and soothing oil. He calls it the Rol-Oyl Cattle Oiler, and his firm, Fleming Manufacturing Co., has sold over 400,000 units.

As soon as he got back to Hastings, Gene called his sister-in-law. "Billee, how about I take that footless goose off your hands? He'll be better off swimming in my pond than tryin' to walk on those sticks of his."

Billee refused. "Even though he can't mate because he can't stand up, Polly is his wife, and I wouldn't separate them," she said.

"I'll take Polly too," Gene proposed. Still his sister-in-law said no. Finally Gene offered to trade two blue-eyed Pomeranian geese for them. Telling him he was crazy to trade valuable geese for a gray one without feet, she relented.

Gene fetched Andy and Polly and turned them loose in his pond. Polly sailed off gracefully. Andy worked his footless stilts as fast as an eggbeater but succeeded only in churning up silt. Gene lifted him out of the pond. "Okay, young fella," he said, "let's see what we can figure out for you."

While examining Andy's stilts, Gene didn't see Polly climb out of the pond. Determined to defend her mate, she grabbed Gene's pants and tugged furiously. "Exile for you, my girl," Fleming decreed, as he shooed her into a shed. "With a little bit of luck, I'll fix you up a proper husband."

Shoes, Gene decided—Andy needed some sort of shoes. In town, Gene bought a pair of white-leather baby shoes, size 0. Andy held still while Gene slipped them over his knobs, laced them, and tied a bow. Then Andy leaned down, untied the bows, and pulled his legs out. So

He didn't mind at all when they crowded around and petted him.

Gene glued the bows to the shoes. Andy fell into the pond, kicked off one of the shoes and, paddling with the other, swam in a circle until Gene caught him.

Gene began experimenting. He placed sponge rubber in the shoes, allowing both soles to lie flat on the ground. He also cut the back of the right shoe so Andy's cocked right leg would fit in and then punched small holes into the soles so water could drain out.

Meanwhile, with Gene busy elsewhere, Andy's life was made miserable by two white Chinese geese that pecked his legs and wings and sent him off cowering. "Never mind, Andy," Gene told him. "One of these days you'll show 'em."

When the shoes were ready, Gene drew little white socks over Andy's knobs, laced the shoes snuggly around his ankles, and glued down the bows. He propped Andy on his feet. The goose sank to the ground helplessly. Unable to rid himself of the shoes, Andy lay on his breast and pushed along the ground with the tips. Gene debated getting him a skateboard, but decided against it.

Instead, he buckled a dog harness around the goose's body and dangled him from a leash like a marionette. "You've got toes now, Andy. Lean into them and take a step." For three hours, Gene bounced Andy on his new feet. "Come on, Andy, you can walk if you think you can. All it takes is believing you can."

Finally, Andy took a tiny step. It wasn't more than four inches, but it was a step. "That's it, Andy!" Gene exclaimed. "You've got it!"

Staggering like a fat baby in diapers, Andy inched around the yard. Gene unhooked the leash. Andy teetered but stayed upright. Now Andy stretched his neck and, lifting his head high, honked almost exultantly. He was six inches taller than he'd ever been before.

Because Andy had never had reason to use them, his ankles were stiff. But he stayed on his feet, and after several days of practice he was strutting around the yard. Gene then released Polly from the shed. She walked straight to Andy and stared at his new white feet. "What do you think, Polly?" Gene asked.

She gave a shake of her head and flounced away as if to say, "He's a silly goose." Suddenly there was a terrific honking. The two Chinese whites were bearing down on Polly and Andy. With a flurry of feathers, Polly fled into the pond, but Andy stood his ground. Rising on the toes of his shoes, he beat the air with his wings and intimidated the Chinese geese into retreat. Then he marched to the pond and launched himself on the water. With his legs stretched out behind him, kicking his "feet" in unison like a paddle-wheel steamer, Andy quickly outdistanced Polly and began swimming circles around her.

The principle of the shoes worked, but the shoes themselves wore out in a month. Since they cost $12.99 a pair and the life expectancy of a goose in captivity is 30 years, Gene figured it would cost almost $4680 to keep Andy on his feet unless he could come up with a substitute. He went to town again and this time returned with a pair of sneakers. They worked perfectly and proved much more durable.

Word got around Hastings that Gene Fleming was buying baby shoes for a goose. The local paper carried a picture of Andy standing tall in his baby shoes, and a staff member at a local school asked Gene if he would bring Andy in to show the children. "Unless," she said, knowing the temperament of geese, "you think he'll snap at them."

"Not Andy," Gene said confidently. "He likes people." He set about fashioning a carrier, bought Andy a new red harness and leash, and made a tape recording of Polly honking. Then off they went to the school.

Andy strutted back and forth in front of the class, showing off how well he could walk. When Gene played the tape of Polly's voice, Andy lifted his head and honked joyously. The children loved it, and he didn't mind at all when they crowded around and petted him.

Gene took Andy to two more grammar schools in Hastings, and now requests are coming in from neighboring towns. "We don't often get a chance to do something really big for our fellow creatures, human or animal," Gene tells the children. "But keep your eyes open for little things you can do, because little things make a big difference. Like the difference shoes have made for Andy."

The letters Gene gets from the children after Andy's visits suggest they understand. "If I find anything that's hurt," one boy wrote, "I'll try to fix him like you fixed Andy." But Gene cherishes most a card from a girl in the second grade. "I love Mr. Fleming," she wrote, "because he gave Andy goose steps."

"It's a funny thing how blessings come in disguise, isn't it, Andy?" Gene mused recently as he drove home with the goose on the seat beside him. "What seems like the worst thing—your being born without feet—turns out to be the best. What other goose gets to wear sneakers to school and be made an honorary member of the Chamber of Commerce public-relations corps?"

Gene reached out to smooth Andy's feathers where the carrier had ruffled them, and Andy gently caught Gene's sleeve in his beak to give it a tweak. Was that a wink or a blink of Andy's shoe-button eyes? Gene is never quite sure. Just in case, he always winks back.

The Pyramids will not last a moment
compared with the daisy.

D. H. LAWRENCE

LURE OF THE DETOUR

BY
NANCY H. BLAKEY

Poet William Stafford once said that we are defined more by the detours and distractions in life than by the narrow road toward goals. I like this image. But then I am a highly distractible person.

Oh, I have goals like everybody else, and I get things done. But it is the crazy asides in a day that lead me to fruitful territory.

Like a good road trip. For my family this means one long and lazy detour after another—a saunter down back roads that eventually lead to the final destination. The lid is off time, and beyond every curve are possibilities. We stop at barn sales, inspect road kills, and buy the world's juiciest peaches at local fruit stands. And because we are unhurried, we talk.

It wasn't always this way for us. We discovered the lush side of road trips quite by accident—or by detour, you could say.

For years we made the nearly 500-mile drive from our home in Seattle to my parents' home in Boise in nine hours. We traveled the way most people do: the fastest, shortest, easiest route. Especially if my husband, Greg, couldn't come and I was alone with four noisy, restless kids who hate confinement and have strong opinions about everything.

Road trips felt risky, so I would drive fast, stopping only when I had to. I'd discipline the kids with my eye on the road and my arm waving into the far reaches of the car. We'd stick to the freeways. We'd count the hours and miles and arrive tired and cranky.

But then Banner was born.

Banner is our sheep. He was rejected by his mama days before a planned trip to Boise. I had two choices: Leave the lamb with my husband, who would have to take him to the office, feed him every two hours, and remember to change his diapers. Or take Banner to Boise with me. Greg made the decision for me.

That is how I found myself on the road with four kids, a baby lamb, five bikes, and nothing but my eternal optimism to see me through. We took the back roads out of sheer necessity. We had to stop every hour and let Banner shake out his long wobbly legs. The kids chased him and one another. They'd get back in the car breathless and energized, smelling fresh from the cold air.

We began to think of ourselves as weird in a wonderful sort of way. While the world was whizzing by, we were not. Instead of pushing through to Boise, in one shot, we stayed in a small motel in Baker, Oregon. This led in the morning to the discovery of a diner that served the most tender and fragrant cinnamon rolls we had ever eaten.

We explored side roads off side roads, surrendering to whim, like grasshopper-catching in waist-high weeds. Even if we simply looked out the car windows at clothes flapping on a line, or baby pigs waddling after their mother, or the rise of a trout on an elbow of creek, it was better than the best ride down the freeway. Here was life. And new horizons.

We eventually arrived at my parents' doorstep astonishingly fresh and full of stories. It had taken us an extra five hours of road time, but heck, we used to spend five hours just recovering.

I grew brave—and a little giddy—with this venture. On the way home I looped through Idaho's panhandle to visit my grandmother. We paused at a hot spring I had raced past heedlessly for years. And I grew creative with my disciplining technique. On an empty stretch of road in eastern Washington, everyone started to bicker. I stopped the car, ordered all kids out, and told them to meet me up ahead. I drove about a mile, parked on the side, and read my book in sweet silence.

That trip with Banner opened our eyes to a world available to anyone reckless enough to idle and putter around. We discovered that we *can* stop at a river just because our toes are hot and the water is cold. The world *can* wait while we pull over to read historical markers along the road, imagining for one brief moment the courage and grit it took to survive a century and a half ago.

Some road trips are by necessity fast and straight. But it took a tiny black lamb to make me realize that a detour may uncover the best part of a journey—and the best part of yourself.

After a visit to the beach, it's hard to believe that we live in a material world.

PAM SHAW

My job was to help capture some birds and that was why I was there

"THERE CAME A CRY OF JOY"

BY
LOREN EISELEY

We entered that southwestern valley through the trailing mists of a spring night. It was a place that looked as though it might never have known the foot of man, but in fact scouts for our expedition had been ahead of us and so we knew all about the abandoned cabin that lay far up on one hillside.

I arrived at the cabin first. From near its entrance I could see our cavalcade—mostly the reflection of truck lights on our collecting tins—winding in and out through the mist below. I stood on a rock a moment looking down and thinking what it cost in money and equipment to capture the past.

We had, in addition, instructions to lay hands on the present. The word had come through to get them alive—birds, reptiles, anything. A zoo somewhere needed restocking. My job was to help capture some birds and that was why I was there before the trucks.

The cabin had not been occupied for years. There were holes in the roof, and birds were roosting in the rafters. A cabin going back to nature in a wild place always draws birds. They find a hole, come inside; then suddenly the place is theirs and man is forgotten.

I got the door open softly, holding a spotlight with which to blind the birds so they couldn't see to get out through the roof. I had a short piece of ladder to put against the far wall, where there was a shelf on which I expected to make the biggest haul. As I pushed the door open, a bird or two stirred but nothing flew.

I padded across the floor and slithered up the ladder till my head and arms were over the shelf. Everything was dark as pitch except for starlight coming through a little hole back of the shelf near the eaves. I reached my arm carefully over in order to be ready to seize whatever was there, and I put the flash on the edge of the shelf, where it would stand by itself. That way I'd be able to use both hands.

I snapped on the flash and sure enough there was a great beating and feathers flying, but instead of my having the birds, they—or rather he—had me. I heard him give one short metallic cry when the light went on and my hand descended on the bird beside him; after that, he was busy digging his claws and beak into my thumb. In the struggle, I knocked the lamp over on the shelf, and his mate got her sight back and whisked neatly through the hole in the roof. It all happened in 15 seconds.

You might think I would have fallen down the ladder, but no, I had a professional assassin's reputation to keep up, and the bird, of course, made the mistake of thinking the hand was the enemy and not the eyes behind it. He chewed my thumb up pretty effectively and lacerated my hand with his claws. But in the end I got him.

He was a sparrow hawk—a fine young male in the prime of life. The little fellow had saved his mate by diverting me, but he made no outcry now, resting hopelessly in my hand, peering toward me in the shadows behind the lamp with a fierce, almost indifferent glance. He

neither gave nor expected mercy, and something out of the high air passed from him to me, stirring a faint embarrassment.

I put the hawk in a box too small to allow him to injure himself by struggle, and walked out to welcome the arriving trucks. In the morning that bird would be just another episode. He would go back in the truck to a small cage in a city where he would spend the rest of his life. And a good thing, too. I sucked my aching thumb and spat out some blood.

In the morning, the mist was gone. The sky was a deep blue, and one could see for miles over the high outcroppings of stone. I was up early and brought the box in which the little hawk was imprisoned out onto the grass where I was building a cage. A wind as cool as a mountain spring ran over the grass. It was a fine day to be alive. I looked up and all around and at the hole in the cabin roof out of which the other little hawk had fled. There was no sign of her. "Probably in the next county by now," I thought. Before beginning work, I decided I'd have a look at my last night's capture.

I got him in my hand with his wings folded properly, careful not to startle him. He lay limp in my grasp. I could feel his heart pound under the feathers, but he only looked beyond me and up—one last look away into a sky so full of light that I could not follow his gaze.

I suppose I must have had an idea then of what I was going to do, but I never let it come up into consciousness. I just reached over and laid the hawk on the grass.

He lay there a long minute without hope, unmoving, his eyes still fixed on that blue vault above him. It must have been that he was already so far away in heart that he never felt the release. He just lay with his breast against the grass.

The second after that long minute he was gone. Like a flicker of light, he vanished with my eyes full on him, gone straight up into that towering emptiness of light that my eyes could scarcely bear to penetrate. For another long moment there was silence. Then, from far up somewhere, a cry came ringing down.

I was young then and had seen little of the world, but when I heard that cry my heart turned over. It was not the cry of the hawk I had captured; for, by shifting my position against the sun, I was now seeing further up. Straight out of the sun's eye, where she must have been soaring restlessly above us for untold hours, hurtled his mate. And from far up, ringing from peak to peak of the summits over us, came a cry of such unutterable and ecstatic joy that it sounds down across the years and tingles among the cups on my quiet breakfast table.

I saw them both now. He was rising fast and they met in a great soaring gyre that turned to a whirling circle and a dance of wings. Once more, just once, their two voices joined in a harsh wild medley of questions and response, struck and echoed against the pinnacles of the valley. Then they were gone forever, into those upper regions beyond the eyes of men.

THE PIG WHO LOVED PEOPLE

BY
JO COUDERT

The phone rang at Bette and Don Atty's house in Johnstown, New York. It was a friend calling to ask if they'd like a pig.

"His name is Lord Bacon. He's four months old, and he's smarter than any dog," the friend said to Don. "He adores people, and with Bette working at home, I thought she might like the company."

For a year Don had stood by helplessly as his wife suffered from agoraphobia, a fear of open spaces and crowds, apparently triggered by stress at work. Even after she had quit her job, just going to the local mall could bring on an anxiety attack. She couldn't leave the house unless Don was with her.

Now Bette was standing nearby, overhearing the conversation, and she shook her head no. "Think about it," Don urged. "It'll be good for you to have a special pet."

Bette recalled reading in one of the many psychology books she had consulted about her condition that caring for another creature strengthens a person's inner being. *But could a pig help my nerves?*

"All right," she said reluctantly. "I suppose some farmer'll take him if we have to get rid of him."

Two hours later the owner delivered Lord Bacon in a wire cage. He was a miniature variety who stood 14 inches high and 24 inches long. Shaped like a root-beer keg on stilts, he weighed 45 pounds.

Don laughed when he saw him. "That snout looks like he ran into a wall doing ninety!" Even Bette joined in: "I've got an old hairbrush with better-looking bristles than these."

When the cage was opened, Lord Bacon trotted out wagging his straight tail, looked around, and headed for Bette. She knelt to greet him. He heaved himself up on his hind legs, laid his head on her shoulder, and kissed her on the cheek with his leathery snout. She looked at the pig and, for the first time in a long time, smiled.

The rest of the day, Bette and Don watched as the pig bustled about, exploring the house. He sat up on his bottom and begged for a treat. He gently chewed on Don's beard when Don put him on his lap. When they whistled, he came to them.

That night the pig tried to follow Bette and Don upstairs, but with his potbelly he couldn't negotiate the steps. Bette made a bed for him in the kitchen, then sat on the floor and stroked him. "It's all right. We'll be here in the morning," she told him.

The next morning, instead of dreading having to face another day, Bette was actually eager to see her new pet. Lord Bacon scrambled to greet her and rubbed against her leg. It was like being massaged with a Brillo pad. From then on, Bette was destined always to have this red rash of affection on her leg.

After breakfast the pig followed Bette into the small home office where she prepared tax returns, and settled down beside her desk. Bette found that when she grew edgy, if she reached down and petted him and said a few words, it made her feel calmer.

Very soon the pig was a member of the household. When Don brought home a doggy bed to put next to Bette's desk, the animal looked it over and decided that, with some alterations, it would do nicely. He planted his hoofs, ripped open the tartan pillow, pulled out the stuffing, and then crawled inside the cover, content.

One evening when Bette and Don drew up their armchairs to watch television, the pig pushed a chair over with his snout and sat up in front of it, as if to say, "Hey, I want to be part of this too." As he watched figures on the screen, his head bobbed from side to side.

Lord Bacon disliked loud noises. Bette's phone hung on a post beside her desk, and the pig figured out that it stopped ringing when Bette picked it up. If Bette wasn't there to answer it immediately, he yanked the receiver off the hook, stood over it, and grunted into the mouthpiece.

I wonder what my clients must think, Bette thought, only half-amused.

One day a client came to see her about his tax return and was so charmed by her pet that he returned later with his children. Soon other neighbors were stopping by to see Lord Bacon. Finding this to be too formidable a name for such a friendly, small pig, the kids took to calling him Pigger, and Pigger he became from then on.

Once when a small group had gathered, Bette felt herself growing tense. Realizing they were all too fascinated by the pig to look at her, however, she began to enjoy the company.

"It's fun coming home from work now," Don told Bette. "The first thing you say is, 'Guess what Pigger did today. He pulled the blankets off the bed,' or whatever, and we get to laughing and it feels like when we were first married."

"You laugh," Bette said, "but it wasn't so funny when he locked me out this morning." Pigger had followed Bette in and out of the house and had watched her close the door behind her. That morning as he went inside, he took the initiative himself—except that the door was on the latch and his mistress was still outside. Luckily, she had a spare key.

More and more Bette realized that Pigger was a superb mimic and would imitate whatever she and Don did. If she shook her head, Pigger would too. If she twirled, Pigger would twirl. Soon Bette was teaching tricks to her pig that few dogs would learn. His reward was dog biscuits.

In Pigger's company Bette was beginning to be more like her old self—so much so that her father tried to persuade her to bring Pigger to a senior-citizens meeting. Bette demurred. "Pigger can run like the wind and feint like a soccer player," she said, "but he hates a leash. He plants his feet and won't walk. I'd look pretty silly, wouldn't I, a grown lady dragging a pig?"

The next night Don came home with a baby stroller. "What's that?" Bette demanded.

"It's a pigmobile, so you can take Pigger to the seniors' meeting." Pigger loved the stroller. He sat up in it, blanket around his shoulders, green visor on his head, as Don pushed him about.

Bette finally agreed to take Pigger to the meeting. Her nerves tightened as she drove up. She turned off the motor and sat in the car, trembling. She stroked Pigger, seat-belted beside her, and felt calmer. *I've got to conquer my fears,* she told herself. *I can't spend the rest of my life being afraid.* She struggled out, settled Pigger in the pigmobile, and wheeled him into the building.

The seniors were intrigued. "What is *that?*" they asked. Bette lifted Pigger to the floor. He immediately singled out the oldest woman and trotted over to nuzzle her cheek. The other seniors broke into laughter and crowded around to pet him.

Bette found herself answering questions, at first haltingly, then with enthusiasm. She told the seniors that pigs are smarter than dogs and twice as clean. "Pigger loves it when I put him into the bathtub once a week for a good scrub," she said.

To show off how smart he was, she called to Pigger and told him he was a handsome hog. Pigger strutted about proudly. Then she scolded him for being piggy. Pigger lowered his head in shame and, for good measure, let his tongue hang out. His audience cheered.

Word got around, and soon Bette and Pigger set out on what Don referred to as pig gigs. At a nearby nursing home, she wheeled Pigger from room to room to visit with the patients. In one, an old woman sat staring at her hands in her lap. Suddenly her head came up, and her face cracked in the beginning of a smile. She held out her hands, then wrapped her arms around herself. "What is it?" Bette asked. "Do you want to hug him?" An aide whispered to Bette that the woman had not smiled, spoken, or taken an interest in anything since her husband died years before.

Keep your love of nature, for that is the true way to understand art more and more.

VINCENT VAN GOGH

Bette picked up Pigger and let the old woman pet him. Pigger stayed as quiet as could be, with his ears cocked and his mouth drawn up in a grin.

On later visits, when Pigger came through the front door in his pigmobile, the call would go out: "Pigger's here!" A commotion would start in the halls—the squeak of wheelchairs, the tap-tap of walkers, the shuffle of slippered feet—as the residents hurried to see him.

The more Bette saw of sick and helpless people, the more thoughts of her own illness faded away. "I used to hate myself," she told Don, "but now I'm beginning to thank God every day for being me. Pigger is my therapy."

One day it occurred to Bette that Pigger might carry a message to schoolchildren. Soon she faced an audience of youngsters and invited them to ask Pigger if he would ever take drugs. Pigger shook his head emphatically while grunting and snorting disgust at the idea. Asked if he'd stay in school and study hard, Pigger bowed low and nodded his head.

The children were curious about what Pigger liked to eat. "Dog biscuits, of course. Also beans, corn, carrots, apples, and Cheerios. But the two things Pigger loves best are popcorn and ice cream. At the Dairy Queen, he gets his own dish of ice cream, which he eats neatly from a spoon," Bette explained.

The kids' comments about Pigger ranged from: "He feels like a pot scrubber," to "He has cute ears," to "He looks like my uncle." One little boy, hugging Pigger, said wistfully, "I wish you could come home with me. I know you'd love me." Bette had to hold firmly on the leash to keep Pigger from following the boy.

Sometimes Bette and Don would be shopping in the supermarket, and from the next aisle a child's voice would ring out: "There's the pig's mother and father!" An embarrassed parent would be dragged over to be introduced to "the pig's family."

When strangers stopped, stared, and asked what Pigger was, Don explained, "To us, he's a pig, but to him, he's people." Sometimes Don quoted Winston Churchill: "Dogs look up to us. Cats look down on us. Pigs treat us as equals." And Pigger would confirm this by grunting.

In one year Bette and Pigger made 95 public appearances together, mostly before old people and children. Bette handled each occasion with poise and flair.

In July of 1990, Pigger was invited to attend the Fulton County, New York, Senior Citizens Annual Picnic. The day before, Bette opened the back door. "Why don't you go out and cool off in your pool, Pigger?" she suggested.

Pigger trotted into the yard, and Bette went back to work. Half an hour later, something made her check on him. He was lying in his favorite napping spot in the shade of a barberry bush. He wasn't breathing.

Bette felt panic coming on. She began to wail. *No, I mustn't carry on. Pigger never liked loud noises.* She phoned the police to come take his body. She called two friends to keep her company until Don got home. Then she knew she was going to make it.

Pigger had succumbed to a pulmonary aneurysm. But Bette has her own theory on why he died. "I think Pigger had a heart so big, it just burst with all that love. He helped me become my old self, and he brightened so many other lives. There'll never be another Pigger."

I get up and I bless the light thin clouds
and the first twittering of birds, and the
breathing air and smiling face of the hills.

GIACOMO LEOPARDI

ONE THAT DIDN'T GET AWAY

BY
WILLIAM J. BUCHANAN

On a Saturday afternoon in 1936, I was sitting against an elm tree listening to the old-timers spin tales. I was ten years old, and my family had recently moved to Eddyville, Kentucky, on the east bank of the Cumberland River. I was wondering whether anything might happen this day that would hold my interest.

Suddenly Luther Oliver ran up hollering about a fish. "Head the size of a mop bucket," he said, gesturing wildly. "Mean, beady eyes."

"What'd you do with 'im?"

"Cut him loose," said Luther. "I got no hankering to be another Jonah."

When the laughter subsided, one old-timer leaned back and said, "Old Whiskers."

Old Whiskers, I learned, was a catfish. "Not a mudcat," the old-timer explained. "Blue," he added, as if to assure me of the fish's aristocratic bloodlines. "Least twenty years old now, I figure it. Top a hundred pounds easy."

Old Whiskers lived in the deepest pool below the dam west of town. The pool was known as Dead Man's Hole, after two unfortunate anglers who pitted their motorboat against the fearsome eddies and were dragged beneath the crushing waters. Thereafter, Dead Man's Hole was fished from the bank.

In the 1930s the Cumberland became a mecca for trophy fishermen, as tales of Old Whiskers spread. Each summer, rods were broken like match sticks, hoop nets ripped apart, 100-pound test lines snapped like cotton thread.

And that's how matters stood three years later when I found myself joined in battle against Old Whiskers—all because Judge Francis Utley won a pool game.

Judge Utley was a charismatic figure. He'd been born in Japan, a fact that added an aura of mystery. When his missionary parents returned to his mother's beloved hometown, young Utley took root. Unlike other small-town boys who longed to explore the world, he found contentment in village life. Often asked why, given his abilities, he didn't seek fortune elsewhere, he always responded: "Eddyville suits me fine."

Endearing him to the young was the fact that he was a master storyteller. He also was the best pool player in the county.

Some of us teenagers were gathered at Charley Clark's Pool Hall one Saturday to watch Luther Oliver try, as he did every weekend, to best the judge at eight ball. After a half-dozen futile games, Luther threw his hands up in despair. As I recall, a couple of us got to speculating on how the judge could do *anything,* even catch the elusive denizen of Dead Man's Hole.

Luther emitted a loud guffaw.

To which the judge responded, "Not an impossible task, for a *real* fisherman."

"That so?" Luther dug into his overalls pocket. "Well, Judge, here's five hard-earned dollars that says you can't." In those Great Depression years, it was a sizable wager.

The judge smiled. "Keep your money for pool lessons, Luther." And with a flick of the wrist, he sank the eight ball in a side pocket.

At that moment Willis Towns walked in. Willis had once hooked Old Whiskers, but lost him when the catfish broke his line. "Well, now," said Willis, as he dug a fiver out of his pocket, "I'll just sweeten the pot a bit on that action, Judge."

Every young eye in the pool hall was on the judge. Extracting a ten from his wallet, he laid it on the counter. "I get . . . seven days?"

"Five," said the challengers.

"Done," said the judge.

He turned to me. "Bill, you got *Little Britches* above or below the dam this year?" *Little Britches* was a small skiff, a birthday present from my parents.

"Below," I said.

The judge nodded. "I'll be calling you." Then to his challengers: "Gentlemen, it's now Saturday. I'll be here no later than Thursday to collect my winnings."

Wednesday morning, with barely 24 hours left, the judge called me. "It's a fine day for fishing, Bill. Meet me in half an hour." The "fine day" was damp and cloudy, the kind when catfish are most active.

I sat in the back while he rowed *Little Britches* to a landing downstream of the treacherous spillway. He stepped onto the bank, grabbed the bow line, and pulled *Little Britches* upstream into the strong white-water current. At a limestone boulder, he stopped and took out a long rope. He tied it around the boulder, then attached the other end to the boat's stern. He fastened a second rope to the bow, and the other end to a willow tree.

The judge came back to the boat and settled in the middle seat. "Sit in back and don't move," he said.

He grabbed an oar and in moments *Little Britches* was caught up in the powerful back-flowing currents. Like a runaway roller coaster, the boat rushed headlong toward the roaring spillway. Reined in by the played-out ropes, however, *Little Britches* came to a halt precisely in the middle of Dead Man's Hole.

The judge had attached a large lead-weighted hook to a 24-inch steel leader. The leader was attached to a strong swivel, which, in turn, was tied to a 30-foot clothesline. Now he tied the clothesline to a deflated bicycle inner tube, then tied the tube to the port oarlock. Finally he fastened his bait—a huge glob of chicken livers sewed inside a gauze bag—to the hook, and lowered it into the water.

No sooner had the hook settled to the bottom than the line shot arrow-straight away from the side of the boat. *Little Britches* listed hard to port. Had it not been for the inner tube, we would have taken on water. The judge called out, "Careful. He'll circle now. We have to keep him counterbalanced."

The line cut through the water in a wide arc. Like many catfish, wise from years of combat, Old Whiskers was trying to wrap the line around the anchor chain. But there was none. Then, 30 feet to port, the mighty catfish surfaced. "What a fish!" the judge exclaimed.

Now, body straight as a torpedo, Old Whiskers began to rotate, whipping the water to a froth. But the swivel between leader and line matched him turn for turn. He couldn't wear the line down.

Tiring, Old Whiskers sounded once again. For what seemed to be an hour, he expended his strength until his tugs grew weaker and the listing of the boat subsided.

The judge donned a pair of leather gloves. "He's ours now," he said triumphantly.

The judge pulled the line slowly, until the giant head broke through the surface. Using a huge gaff, he pulled the fish partway out of the water. Then, grasping the base of the erect dorsal fin, he lifted Old Whiskers into the boat.

Old Whiskers was indeed a sight. Three feet long and with a girth of at least 30 inches, he almost filled the bottom of the boat between the middle and rear seats.

Uncharacteristically quiet, the judge sat staring at the vanquished fish. Removing a glove, he ran his hand down the length of Old Whiskers's body, as if caressing a beloved pet. "What a *magnificent* specimen." There was a strange tone in his voice. "Help me get him on this middle seat, so I can measure him properly."

Nature is an excellent sedative. It makes a man carefree. And being carefree is of the essence in this world.

ANTON CHEKHOV

"We oughta do that on shore," I suggested.

The judge ignored me. Grasping the fish in the mouth with his gloved hand, placing his other hand behind the upright dorsal fin, he pulled while I pushed until Old Whiskers lay stretched on his fat belly across the middle seat, close to the oarlock. "Better move him up," I said. "If he gets his tail against something he'll flop overboard."

"Oh? Sure." The judge helped me slide the huge body forward. "Hold him there," he said.

The judge moved toward the bow to get his measuring tape. Suddenly he lost his balance and fell back, his right hand splayed flat precisely at the base of Old Whiskers's tail. It was all the crafty fish needed. With his last bit of strength, he planted his forked tail against the judge's stiffened arm and gave a mighty shove. Old Whiskers plunged over the side.

"Oh!" I cried in anguish. "The hook! Bait the hook!"

With perfect balance now, the judge moved to the middle seat. "It's no use, Bill. He won't strike again today . . . perhaps never again." I swear there was a twinkle in his eye. For some odd reason he seemed at peace. On the trip back he swore me to silence. "No one would believe us, anyway."

Next day at Clark's Pool Hall the judge paid off his debts. "Gentlemen, you were right. No one will ever land that great fish." With a sly wink at me, he left.

Then it hit me. If Judge Utley, the best fisherman in these parts, couldn't catch Old Whiskers, who else would even try? By keeping his accomplishment secret, the judge would assure that Old Whiskers would remain in his rightful place, forever free.

As far as anyone knows, Old Whiskers lived out the remainder of his life at the bottom of Dead Man's Hole. And Judge Utley finished out his days in Eddyville.

Me, I would eventually wander the globe—even, like the judge, living for a while in Japan. But my thoughts return often to my cherished small-town roots, and the day I witnessed a remarkable character perform an act of love for a magnificent fish.

BO'S WORLD

BY
JOE KIRKUP

Most of my memories of Vietnam are the kind that jerk my breath away at 3:00 A.M. and leave me clenching my fists, waiting for the blessed light of dawn. We all made choices we now must live with. How many bullets versus how much water? When the rescue chopper says "only three" and there are four of you, do you leave a guy or "lock and load" on the pilot? Worst of all, when it's dark and nobody can help, do you let some mangled kid die slowly or just get it over with? In all the darkness of that time, however, there was one bright spot: a big German shepherd named Bo.

Bo was a scout dog for my infantry unit. His mission was to sniff out Viet Cong guerrillas, their tunnels, ammo caches, and booby traps. Like the rest of us, he was a soldier on the outside and a puppy in his heart.

Occasionally, our unit would stop for a few days to guard some smoldering mechanized unit or back up a Special Forces team. While we waited, Bo would entertain us with his skills. His handler would tie a thin monofilament across a path, then dare guys to step over it. Bo's job was to stop us. He'd been taught it was better to eat one GI than let him trigger a mine that popped into the air and detonated at the level of everybody's head.

I would pet Bo and let him begin eating my C-rations. Then I'd start toward the string. Bo was never won over by my ham steak. As I approached the tripwire, he'd race ahead, then turn toward me, flattening his radar-station ears and rolling gravy-moistened lips. Bone-crushing teeth would appear. His huge torso would sink into a crouch as he prepared to spring. In 'Nam we dealt with pretty scary stuff, but when Bo told you to stop, no one had the guts to take a step.

The minute I backed off, Bo and I would be pals again. "Sit, Bo. You want a goody?" Sure he did. In those big brown eyes you could read his thoughts: *I'm glad I didn't have to kill this jerk before I got the rest of his C-rats.*

One steamy, miserable day my unit was moving through light jungle and tall trees. I was fourth from point. Bo and his handler were behind me.

Gunshots, their sharpness blunted by the smothering humidity, exploded around us. We hit the vine-covered jungle floor. "In the trees! In the trees!" someone hissed.

More shots came, louder now. Beside me, Bo flinched. I emptied three 20-round clips in the direction of the noise. My frantic and scruffy peers did likewise. When the smoke cleared, a body was hanging out of a tree.

Bo seemed all right. We made him roll over and stand up. Then I saw that line of slick, dark blue-red we all knew too well.

A bullet had pierced Bo's foreleg. It appeared to be a clean hole, bleeding only slightly. When I patted him, he wagged his tail. His sad, intelligent eyes seemed to be saying, "It's okay, Joe. I'm not important. I'm just here to protect you."

A chopper took Bo away. As I smoothed his fur good-bye, I wondered if they would send the big guy home. But in a few weeks, to my joy and sorrow, he was back.

Midsummer. We were 1000 meters from a huge field outside a tiny hamlet, Sui Tres. In the field was an artillery unit. Around them were 2500 VC. Our job was to shoot our way through and secure the howitzer guys.

The night before, we slept on the jungle floor, lying with our heads on our helmets and trying not to notice what crawled over us. Just before dawn, the unsteady rumble of machine-gun and heavy-weapons fire erupted from the direction of Sui Tres. Time to face the devil.

I put on my helmet and grabbed my gear. Bo wandered over to see if we had time for breakfast. Around me the dark jungle was filled with muttered curses and rustling equipment.

Suddenly Russian-made rockets streaked through the treetops overhead. I heard what sounded like escaping steam, followed by a long moment of silence. Then deafening, lung-crushing thunder.

Dust filled the air. I was facedown on the ground, not knowing how I got there. People were screaming for medics. My helmet, split open by shrapnel, no longer fit on my head.

Through the confusion, I saw Bo's long black tail wagging. He was crouched beside his handler, waiting for orders. But the young soldier's right shoulder and most of his chest were gone. White dust covered his corpse and the dog beside him.

I pulled Bo gently toward me and stroked the fur on his back. Sticky liquid covered my hand and ran down the side of his body. A tiny piece of shrapnel had penetrated his back below the spine. He seemed not to notice, and again pulled toward his handler. "He didn't make it," I told Bo, holding the dog against my chest. "He just didn't make it."

Each GI was issued a large cloth bandage. The rule was to use your buddy's bandage for him and save yours for yourself. Bo didn't have a bandage, so I wrapped him in mine.

We put the dead and wounded—humans and canine—on choppers and went on to kill 641 VC before the day was over. I never saw Bo again.

September 18, 1967. I was processing out of 'Nam. Malaria had reduced me from 165 to 130 pounds. I looked and felt like a corpse in combat boots. My heart was filled with death: the smell, the look, the wrenching finality of it. After 11 months and 29 days, it was time to go.

Standing in line, I began talking to the guy in front of me. He'd been a dog handler, he said. Now he was going home to his family's farm in Iowa. "It's a beautiful place," he said. "I never thought I'd live to see it again."

I told him about the scout dog I'd befriended—describing the huge, courageous shepherd and how he'd been shot. The soldier's next words took my breath away.

"You mean Bo!" he exclaimed.

"Yeah, how'd you know?"

"They gave him to me after my dog got killed."

For a moment I was happy. Then two miserable thoughts popped into my brain. First, I'd have to ask what had happened to Bo. Second, this handler was on his way home, leaving that loyal mutt to stay here until his luck ran out.

"So," I said hesitantly, staring at the toe of my boot, "what happened to that dog?"

The soldier lowered his voice the way people do when they have bad news. "He's gone."

I was so sick of death I thought I would throw up. Nothing seemed worth the life of that beautiful animal. I just wanted to sit down on the floor and cry. I guess the guy noticed my clenched fists and the wetness of my eyes. After looking around nervously, he lowered his voice again.

"Not dead, man," he said. "*Gone.* I got my company commander to fill out a death certificate, and we sent Bo back to my parents. He's been there for two weeks. Bo is back in Iowa."

What that skinny farm kid and his commanding officer did may not mean much to all those antiwar college kids who now control the newspapers and TV. And it may not have had the impact of the choices made by the now-remorseful Robert McNamara.

But it represents what was really in all our hearts. Of all the decisions made in Vietnam, this is the one I can live with.

Climb the mountains and get their good tidings. Nature's peace will flow into you as sunshine flows into trees. The winds will blow their freshness into you, and the storms their energy, while cares will drop off like falling leaves.

JOHN MUIR

THE POWER OF HERCULES

BY
BARBARA BARTOCCI

Hercules entered our lives one April Sunday as we picnicked in the park. Andy, my tow-headed eleven-year-old, found him.

I was pouring lemonade when I heard Andy's shout. He ran toward us, holding what looked like a long, crooked stick. Then the stick wriggled and my lemonade splashed across the picnic table.

"But Mom!" Andy cried. "It's only a garter snake. May I keep him? Please?"

My instinct was "No!" But the look in Andy's eyes made me hesitate. Andy was the youngest of my three children, and I worried about him. At four, he'd required surgery on his ears and subsequent speech therapy. A year later, his father died; the same year, doctors diagnosed learning disabilities. He had needed special schools in early grades and still required a tutor. And, like many learning-disabled children, he had grown up feeling "different" and "dumb," even though he was intelligent.

"He has to grow into his own learning power," was the way one doctor had put it.

Lonely children often gravitate to animals, I've heard, maybe because animals offer unconditional acceptance. From an early age, Andy possessed an affinity for animals. Growling dogs would wag their tails at his approach. Hissing cats would purr. But dogs and cats were not allowed in our apartment complex.

I looked from Andy's pleading eyes to the unblinking eyes of the snake. Its tongue flicked at me, and I shuddered.

"Where would you keep it?"

"In my aquarium. I'll put a lid on and never ever let it bother you, Mom." He held the striped, black snake up to his face. "Please, Mom. Please?"

I'm still not sure why I said yes. But Hercules, as Andy named him with a flourish, came home with us.

Andy set to work at once, cleaning the 20-gallon aquarium, lining it with rocks and dirt, setting a branch upright in one corner for Hercules to climb on, installing a light bulb for warmth.

I admired Andy's industry and, once Hercules was safely behind glass, I could even admire the long, striped snake. In the sunlight, his scales danced and glittered, the way sunlight will catch on a dragonfly's wing.

"He's not trying to sting you," said Andy, when I jerked back from Hercules's flicking tongue. "Snakes use their tongues to sense things around them."

To a boy with dyslexia, reading can be an excruciating task. Andy had never read for fun, even though his tutor told us he had overcome his early handicaps. But after Hercules's arrival, Andy checked out every book on snakes in the library. We were amazed at all he learned.

Even more amazing were the changes in Andy, especially after his sixth-grade teacher invited Hercules to school. Andy was smaller than most of his classmates, but I saw his shoulders straighten as he proudly carried the snake to school.

Hercules spent all spring in the classroom, under Andy's charge, and adapted well. Before long, Andy had only to stick his hand in the aquarium for Hercules to slither to his outstretched fingers and glide smoothly up his arm. On the playground, he looped gracefully around Andy's neck, basking in the warm Kansas sunshine, his tongue flicking Andy's cheek.

Hercules returned home when school ended to be joined, for Andy's birthday, by a pair of boa constrictors he named Mabel and Sam.

The boas were young, about 18 inches long, and beautifully mottled in rich shades of brown and tan.

"How do you know they're male and female?" I asked.

"I just know," said Andy confidently. "I'm going to put myself through college by selling baby boas."

College! I marveled again at the changes the snakes had wrought. Here was Andy, who had thought he was "dumb," suddenly talking about college.

As summer veered toward autumn, Herc became Andy's near-constant companion. Often, when Andy went out on his bicycle, Herc rode with him, sometimes wrapped around the handlebars, other times tucked into Andy's drawstring snake bag.

Early one August Sunday a violent shriek pierced the air. Andy stood in the driveway, clutching Hercules. "Herc got spoked!" he gasped.

Somehow the snake bag had become tangled in Andy's bicycle spokes. The result was a punctured snake. Hercules lay unblinking after being wrapped frantically in black friction tape. For the next 24 hours, Andy watched and worried.

I'll never forget Doctor Guglielmino's surprise on Monday when he opened his door to a boy holding out a bandaged garter snake.

"W-will he die?"

The veterinarian coughed. "This is my-uh-first-uh-snake patient," he admitted, as he gingerly unwrapped, then rewrapped the tape. "I think we should let nature take its course."

Hercules survived.

Seventh grade is a tough year for kids, and for shy, insecure Andy, starting junior high could have been a nightmare. But now there was a difference.

I remembered what Andy's teacher had told us on the last day of grade school: "Hercules has given Andy value in his own eyes. For the first time he has something no one else has—something others admire. That's a new feeling for Andy. A good feeling."

In seventh grade, too, the snakes provided him with a sense of self. The lonely boy of a year ago smiled now. He held his head high and stepped confidently into the crowded school hall, knowing that the other kids whispered of him, "He's the guy with the snakes."

The snakes were a regular part of our lives now. When Hercules disappeared from the bathroom one day, after Andy had let him out to exercise, the whole family pitched in for the snake hunt. We found him in the closet, wrapped cozily around one of Andy's sneakers.

And we all watched, fascinated, when Hercules shed his skin, slithering out with a smooth, fluid motion to leave behind the old skin perfectly intact, while his new scales glowed with youth and promise. Carefully Andy collected the old skin and placed it in the shoe box where he kept his valuables.

We never learned what sent Hercules into convulsions that spring. As far as we could tell, nothing had changed in his environment. But one Friday afternoon, Andy ran to me screaming, "Hurry! Something's wrong with Herc!"

Mabel and Sam lay quietly curled in their corner of the aquarium. But Hercules writhed and jumped. His tongue flailed the air wildly.

I grabbed my car keys while Andy wrestled Hercules into the snake bag. Herc thumped and twisted as though filled with evil spirits.

Doctor Guglielmino injected some cortisone, and it seemed to work. Gradually Hercules grew calmer. Andy gently stroked his snake, and slowly Hercules reached up and flicked Andy's cheek with his tongue. He flowed again into a graceful loop around Andy's neck.

For several weeks thereafter, Hercules seemed fine. But then the convulsions returned, and we raced to the vet's for another shot of cortisone. Once again, Hercules recovered.

But the third time was too much. Although the cortisone quieted the massive convulsion, it was apparent as we drove home that Hercules was dying. His long, lean body lay limp in Andy's lap. His scales, instead of catching the light, were clouded and gray.

He tried to lift his head as Andy stroked his back, but the effort was more than he could manage. His tongue flickered once, weakly, like a candle flame about to go out. And then he was still.

Tears rolled silently down Andy's cheeks. And mine.

To the eyes of the man of imagination, nature is imagination itself.

WILLIAM BLAKE

It would be another year before Andy would blossom, seemingly overnight, into the six feet of linebacker's build that would carry him through high school. Today he's a college student, making good grades in the tough premed program required for veterinary school.

Andy never did raise baby boas, but Mabel and Sam stayed with us all through high school, bequeathed, at the end, to Andy's biology class. They never took the place of Hercules, though.

In Andy's top drawer, there is still a dried snake skin. Before he left for college last year, I suggested it might be time to throw it out.

Andy looked at me in horror. "Don't you dare!"

He touched the skin gently. "Ol' Herc . . . he was sure one splendid snake, wasn't he?"

Yes, he was. He gave a shy, lonely boy the first intimation of all he was—and all he could be.

Ol' Herc . . . I thank you.

WALTER AND THE GEESE

BY
H. GORDON GREEN

For the first 12 years after I took over our farm, there wasn't a goose on the place. And then one June morning a sad-faced lad of ten came up the road with five downy goslings peering over the rim of a basket.

"My old man says we got to move again," he said. "To town this time. These here's pets. They'd follow me to hell an' gone."

I paid $10 for the lot, and before the day was out they were following *me* to hell an' gone. It could be quite funny to have them always tangled around your feet if you could take the time to laugh at it. But it was downright exasperating when you had to get somewhere.

Soon the goslings grew saucy, roamed farther afield, and their feather stubs began to stab through the yellow and gray down. They became gawky and insatiably curious.

Across the road my neighbor, Walter, began to watch the goslings instead of television. Walter was an invalid with an ailing heart. "I've seen geese before," he said, "but these are different. They're really clowns, these. Sometimes I sit here half the afternoon just laughing at them."

He'd been an outdoorsman all of his life, and I'd never known anyone who could read animals so well. A man who used to be so very much alive couldn't have many things left to laugh at when he had to be content with watching the world through his window.

"And they're clever, too!" Walter told me. "You know what they do now every time the dogs come near them? They beat it for your porch and line up outside the front door. They know bloody well a dog isn't going to try any shenanigans there!"

It seemed no time at all before the geese were acting as though they owned the place. They threatened, bullied, shrieked obscenities at every new face. One September morning I found them in Walter's garden and they had made a mess of it. I wanted to pay for it, but Walter wouldn't hear of it. "Could of stopped them myself if I'd wanted to," he said. "But they were havin' an awful lot of fun thinkin' they were deep in sin. And besides, the doc had me in for a checkup yesterday. He told me not to get upset over things."

Looking at Walter, I thought he was much grayer than usual. "How did the checkup go?" I asked.

"The doc switched me onto a new medicine," he said. "But he told me not to start readin' any more continued magazine stories."

It was awkward trying to laugh with him. A man like Walter ought to live forever.

November blew down on us, and one night when the wind was throwing the moon around, my geese began to holler. A minute later my phone rang. "You wonder what's got into your geese?" Walter asked. "There's a flock of Canadas goin' over. Guess yours are tryin' to flag them down."

When I went outside I could barely see the Canadas. There were 30 or 40 of them maybe. In a few minutes Walter came over and we

watched them together. Meanwhile, my five earthbound geese were tilting their heads at the sky and calling at the top of their lungs.

They kept up their silly calling long after the sky was quiet and empty. We turned to go in for coffee and Walter said, "Something kind of special about the first flock goin' over. Kind of sad, too. As if you know it's gettin' near the end."

The way he said it made me feel awkward again.

One night Walter rang me out of my sleep. "You want to see some fun?" he asked. "Well, there's a flock of honkers down in front of your woods. They just landed. I'm sure of it! And your geese are headed back to see them."

I'm a bird lover, but to tell the truth, I don't love them enough to let them dump me out of a warm bed on a November night. I went because of Walter mainly. He couldn't dare a trip like that himself, and he would want to know what happened.

The ground was silver-plated with frost, and the moonlight was so strong your shadow walked along with you. But I could hear the Canadas a long time before I could see them. I could also hear my own geese up ahead of me somewhere, yelling hellos as they went. I had never known them to go so far from home before, and when I was finally able to see them I began to get excited, too. I began to wonder how I would feel if, on some otherworldly night, I had the chance to step back across a million years and meet my ancestors face to face.

The Canadas paid no attention at first. Maybe they were talking too much to hear the other geese. Then suddenly, just as I got my first hazy look at the flock, they froze, and the only sound left in the night was that of my geese hysterically hollering hello. I saw the Canadas snapping to attention, their necks stiff as old mullein stalks, and then the air was full of wings. They lifted over the woods and out of sight.

"A big flock like that could be the last roundup," Walter said later.

He was right. We had seen the last of the Canadas and also the last of autumn. Next day the first flints of sleet came bounding down, and before the week was out the snow had covered everything but the goldenrod along the headlands. My geese had to give up foraging now and they parked on the front doorstep. They seemed strangely quiet.

I didn't share Walter's excitement when he called me one night to tell me that those damfool geese of mine were now teaching themselves to fly. "Craziest thing you ever saw," he said. "Every morning about sunup they line up over in the corner of your front pasture. And then they rev up and point their noses into the wind and go hell-a-whoopin' across the whole bloody field. And I swear to God they're gettin' now so's their feet don't hardly touch bottom!"

Nothing ever comes of such games, I thought. Domestic geese, like the humans who think they own them, are too soft and too heavy to return to Eden.

Then one morning when I was rounding the corner of the barn with a couple of pails of calf feed, I met a goose who was sufficiently airborne to knock my hat off. He and the others were ridiculously awkward at first. Once a gander struck my telephone wire so hard I was sure he had broken his neck, but two days later he was lifting higher than ever. Even after the geese could gain enough altitude to clear the treetops, they were still making comical mistakes, landing in the middle of the cattle, or on the roof of the barn and then tobogganing down over the edge and onto the manure pile below. "It's a wonder they don't massacre themselves," Walter said.

Then, suddenly, the awkward comedy was over. Their flying became sure and triumphantly beautiful, and when they floated by over my head, there was a grace and a majesty to them that made my throat tighten.

Walter said he saluted every time they went by his window. He spent a good deal of time on his back now, but he had rolled his cot alongside the window so he still saw more of the geese than I did. And it was he who reported the tragedy to me.

"Better go out and look behind your lilac bush," he told me one night when I got home. "Your Springer and your Pointer—well, the geese came down right in front of them, and they sort of ganged up on one. It couldn't lift out of the way fast enough, I guess."

True wisdom consists in not departing from nature and in molding our conduct according to her laws and model.

SENECA

Because I was pretty sure those dogs would do the same thing again first chance they had, I took my pail of oats into the machine shed that night, and when the geese followed me I shut the door on them. "That's all for this year," I told them. "You'll just have to stay put."

I hadn't been thinking about Walter at all, I guess, that night. But one morning, when I went in to split some kindling for him, I noticed that his couch was no longer by the window.

"My God, but the days do be long now!" he told me.

He was so thin-faced and gray I found myself looking off around the room instead, but that didn't help either because everywhere you looked there was something more of the outdoors he had always liked so much. Snowshoes, pack harness, pelts, horn, feathers, a collection of eggs. "I keep thinkin' about them geese of yours," he said. "Judas Priest, but I do miss seein' them go by the window and thumbing their arses at me! I keep thinkin' if I was a goose and you was to give me the choice between bein' a safe prisoner or flyin' free, and maybe gettin' my neck bit off, I know what I'd choose!"

Next morning I let the geese out of the shed and I locked up the dogs. And the geese took off and went shrieking around the farm and over the house and through the trees till I thought they would drop from sheer fatigue.

"Hell no, they're not *tired!"* Walter said. "Can't you hear them laughing up there?"

He had his couch smack-tight to the window again. *I'll go in one morning,* I thought, *and find him dead on that couch.*

I was wrong about that. They found him one soft, misty, green morning in April about halfway back to the woods. He had a little pack on his back and a pair of field glasses.

Maybe, if some of you happen to cross over before I do, you might tell Walter for me that the geese are still flying free. He shouldn't be hard to find, because if things are like they say they are over there, this time he must have had no trouble making it all the way to the woods.

ACKNOWLEDGMENTS

All the stories in *The Blessings of Nature* previously appeared in *Reader's Digest* magazine. We would like to thank the following contributors and publishers for permission to reprint material:

Articles

A Hummingbird's Magic by Norma Lee Browning. "HE SAW A HUMMINGBIRD," copyright © 1978 by Norma Lee Browning. Published by Dutton, a division of Penguin Putnam.

Lampo, The Dog Who Rode Trains by Elvio Barlettani. "LAMPO, IL CANE VIAGGIATORE," copyright © 1962 by Garzanti Libri, S.p.A.

Where the Sun Spilled Gold by Jaroldeen Edwards. "THINGS I WISH I'D KNOWN SOONER," copyright © 1997 by Jaroldeen Edwards. Published by Pocket Books, a division of Simon & Schuster Inc.

When the Moon Follows Me by Mary E. Potter. © 1988 by Mary E. Potter. The Berkshire Eagle (October 18, '88).

Sure Is Cold by Nick Jans. "A PLACE BEYOND: FINDING HOME IN ARCTIC ALASKA," copyright © 1996 by Nick Jans. Published by Graphic Arts Center Publishing.

What I Learned on the Road by Charles Kuralt. From "ON THE ROAD WITH CHARLES KURALT" by Charles Kuralt, copyright © 1985 by CBS Inc. Used by permission of G.P. Putnam's Sons, a division of Penguin Putnam Inc.

"Have You Seen The Tree?" by Robert S. Kyff. © 1990 by Robert S. Kyff. Hartford Courant (October 21, '90).

Great Skunk Caper by Bob Noonan. © 1987 by Bob Noonan. The Trapper (April '87).
A Boy and His Cat by Judith S. Johnessee. © 1994 by The Associated Press. AP Newsfeatures (November 27, '94).
Where the Sun Always Rises by Marnie O. Mamminga. © 1994 by Marnie O. Mamminga. Detroit Free Press Magazine (August 7, '94).
Lure of the Detour by Nancy H. Blakey. © 1995 by Nancy H. Blakey. Eastside Parent (July '95).
"There Came a Cry of Joy" by Loren Eiseley. From "THE IMMENSE JOURNEY" by Loren Eiseley, copyright © 1946, 1950, 1951, 1953, 1955, 1956, 1957 by Loren Eiseley. Used by permission of Random House, Inc.
Bo's World by Joe Kirkup. © 1995 by Joe Kirkup. Northeast Magazine (May 14, '95).
Walter and the Geese by H. Gordon Green. From "DIARY OF A DIRTY OLD MAN," copyright © 1974 by the Estate of H. Gordon Green. Originally published by McClelland & Stewart Ltd., Canada.

Quotations

John Muir, "MY FIRST SUMMER IN THE SIERRA" (Houghton Mifflin Co.); *Rachel Peden* in Indianapolis Star (February 19, '75); *Luther Burbank,* "HAPPY THOUGHTS" by Louise Backelder (Peter Pauper Press); *Max Lucado,* "THE GREAT HOUSE OF GOD" by Max Lucado, copyright © 1997, Word Publishing, Nashville, Tennessee. All rights reserved; *Ken Weber* in Providence Rhode Island Journal-Bulletin; *Alan Hovhaness* in the New York Times (August 3, '86); *Martin Buxbaum* in TABLE TALK; *Paul Scott Mowrer,* "THE HOUSE OF EUROPE" (Houghton Mifflin Co.); *Henry James* quoted by Edith Wharton. Reprinted with the permission of Scribner, a Division of Simon & Schuster, Inc., from A BACKWARD GLANCE by Edith Wharton. Copyright © 1933, 1934 by The Curtis Publishing Co., copyright renewed © 1961, 1962; *Hal Borland,* "SUNDIAL OF THE SEASONS" (Lippincott); *D. H. Lawrence,* "D. H. LAWRENCE AND ITALY" (Viking Penguin). Biblical Scriptures are from the "REVISED STANDARD VERSION OF THE BIBLE," National Council of the Churches of Christ in the USA (Thomas Nelson).

Photo Credits

All photographs are from Photodisc unless otherwise credited below:

Cover: Geoff Dore/Stone; title page: Carol Havens/Stone; pp. 2-3: Bob and Carol Calhoun/Bruce Coleman; pp. 10-11: Ian Clark/International Stock; pp. 18-19: Eunice

Harris/Photo Researchers; p. 23: Larry Allan/Bruce Coleman; pp. 26-27: M. Toyoura/Photonica; p. 29: George Ancona/International Stock; p. 33: First Light/Image State; p. 37: Wayne Lank Inen/Bruce Coleman; pp. 46-47: Ron Morsch/Stock Market; p. 49: Tom Stewart/Stock Market; p. 56: Joseph Nettis/Photo Researchers; pp. 64-65: Zefa/Bruce Coleman; p. 67: Bob Frith/International Stock; p. 69: Sekai Bunka/Panoramic Images; p. 72: Sekai Bunka/Panoramic Images; p. 77: Thomas Winz/Panoramic Images; p. 83: Norbert Wu/Peter Arnold; p. 87: Frank Krahmer/Bruce Coleman; pp. 88-89: Robert Dowling/Corbis; p. 91: Mark Turnsek/Stone; pp. 94-95: Kamil Vognar/Photonica; p. 105: T. Sawada/Photonica; p. 107: Kevin Byron/Bruce Coleman; p. 116: Greg Huglin/Image State; p. 121: Bob and Carol Calhoun/Bruce Coleman; p. 128: E. R. Degginger/Bruce Coleman; pp. 130-131: Rolf Kopfle/Bruce Coleman; p. 132: George di Sario/Stock Market; p. 134: Alan Caruthers/Photo Researchers; p. 147: Douglas Walker/Masterfile; p. 153: Image State; pp. 158-159: Tom Brakefield/Bruce Coleman; p. 161: Karen McGougan/Bruce Coleman; p. 169: Barbara Williams; pp. 172-173: Lew Lause/Superstock; p. 174: Chris Volk/Superstock; p. 183: Erwin and PeggyBauer/Bruce Coleman; p. 189: Ron Thoman/FPG; p. 191: Frank Krahmer/Bruce Coleman; p. 196: Art Wolfe/Stone; pp. 208-209: Daniel Zupanc/Bruce Coleman; p. 215: Kristian Hilson/Stone; pp. 220-221: Erwin and Peggy Bauer/Bruce Coleman; p. 223: Hans Reinhard/Bruce Coleman; pp. 226-227: Gerard Lacz/Peter Arnold; p. 229: Gerard Lacz/Peter Arnold; pp. 232-233: Paul Vozdic/Photonica; p. 235: William Mullins/Photo Researchers; pp. 238-239: Gary Crandall/Envision; p. 241: David Madison/Bruce Coleman.

Carousel Research: Laurie Platt Winfrey, Van Bucher, Cristian Pena, Peter Tomlinson